THE IMPORTANCE OF

Franklin D. Roosevelt

These and other titles are included in The Importance Of biography series:

Maya Angelou
Louis Armstrong
James Baldwin
Lucille Ball
The Beatles
Alexander Graham Bell
Napoleon Bonaparte
Julius Caesar
Rachel Carson
Charlie Chaplin
Charlemagne
Winston Churchill
Christopher Columbus
Leonardo da Vinci
James Dean
Charles Dickens
Walt Disney
Dr. Seuss
F. Scott Fitzgerald
Anne Frank
Benjamin Franklin
Mohandas Gandhi
John Glenn
Jane Goodall

Martha Graham
Lorraine Hansberry
Ernest Hemingway
Adolf Hitler
Thomas Jefferson
John F. Kennedy
Martin Luther King Jr.
Bruce Lee
John Lennon
Douglas MacArthur
Margaret Mead
Golda Meir
Mother Teresa
John Muir
Richard M. Nixon
Pablo Picasso
Edgar Allan Poe
Queen Elizabeth I
Jonas Salk
Margaret Sanger
William Shakespeare
Frank Sinatra
Tecumseh
Simon Wiesenthal

THE IMPORTANCE OF

Franklin D. Roosevelt

by Michael V. Uschan

Lucent Books, an Imprint of The Gale Group
10911 Technology Place, San Diego, CA 92127

To Kathy Bates:
Hope you enjoy the book!

Library of Congress Cataloging-in-Publication Data

Uschan, Michael V., 1948–
    Franklin D. Roosevelt / by Michael V. Uschan.
        p.   cm. — (The importance of)
Includes bibliographical references and index.
    Summary: Profiles the life and work of Franklin D. Roo-
sevelt, discussing his early education, illness, political career,
achievements during the Great Depression, and legacy.
        ISBN 1-56006-967-8 (hardback : alk. paper)
        1. Roosevelt, Franklin D. (Franklin Delano), 1882–1945—
Juvenile literature. 2. Presidents—United States—Biography—
Juvenile literature. [1. Roosevelt, Franklin D. (Franklin Delano),
1882–1945. 2. Presidents.]   I. Title. II. Series.
     E807 .U83   2002
        973.917'092—dc21

2001005791

Contents

Foreword

THE IMPORTANCE OF biography series deals with individuals who have made a unique contribution to history. The editors of the series have deliberately chosen to cast a wide net and include people from all fields of endeavor. Individuals from politics, music, art, literature, philosophy, science, sports, and religion are all represented. In addition, the editors did not restrict the series to individuals whose accomplishments have helped change the course of history. Of necessity, this criterion would have eliminated many whose contribution was great, though limited. Charles Darwin, for example, was responsible for radically altering the scientific view of the natural history of the world. His achievements continue to impact the study of science today. Others, such as Chief Joseph of the Nez Percé, played a pivotal role in the history of their own people. While Joseph's influence does not extend much beyond the Nez Percé, his nonviolent resistance to white expansion and his continuing role in protecting his tribe and his homeland remain an inspiration to all.

These biographies are more than factual chronicles. Each volume attempts to emphasize an individual's contributions both in his or her own time and for posterity. For example, the voyages of Christopher Columbus opened the way to European colonization of the New World. Unquestionably, his encounter with the New World brought monumental changes to both Europe and the Americas in his day. Today, however, the broader impact of Columbus's voyages is being critically scrutinized. *Christopher Columbus,* as well as every biography in The Importance Of series, includes and evaluates the most recent scholarship available on each subject.

Each author includes a wide variety of primary and secondary source quotations to document and substantiate his or her work. All quotes are footnoted to show readers exactly how and where biographers derive their information, as well as provide stepping stones to further research. These quotations enliven the text by giving readers eyewitness views of the life and times of each individual covered in The Importance Of series.

Finally, each volume is enhanced by photographs, bibliographies, chronologies, and comprehensive indexes. For both the casual reader and the student engaged in research, The Importance Of biographies will be a fascinating adventure into the lives of people who have helped shape humanity's past and present, and who will continue to shape its future.

Important Dates in the Life of Franklin D. Roosevelt

1928
On November 6 Roosevelt is elected governor of New York.

1882
On January 30 Franklin Delano Roosevelt is born at Springwood, the family estate in Hyde Park, New York.

1917
On April 6 the United States enters World War I.

1932
Roosevelt is elected president, defeating incumbent Herbert Hoover.

1912
Roosevelt is reelected to the New York state Senate.

1921
Roosevelt is stricken with polio while vacationing at Campobello Island.

1905
On March 17 Roosevelt marries Eleanor Roosevelt, a fifth cousin once removed.

1903
Roosevelt graduates from Harvard.

1880	1885	1890	1895	1900	1905	1910	1915	1920	1925	1930

1900
Roosevelt enters Harvard; his father, James, dies on December 8.

1930
Roosevelt is reelected governor.

1913
Roosevelt becomes the assistant secretary of the navy.

1904
Roosevelt enters Columbia Law School; he studies there for three years but never gets his degree.

1924
At the Democratic National Convention, Roosevelt makes his most important political appearance since contracting polio, delivering a stirring speech nominating Alfred Smith for president.

1910
Roosevelt is elected to the New York State Senate on November 8.

1920
Roosevelt runs as vice president on the Democratic ticket with James M. Cox; the Republican ticket of Warren Harding and Calvin Coolidge win the election.

1933
On February 15 President-elect Roosevelt is shot at in an assassination attempt; on March 4 Roosevelt is inaugurated as president; on March 9 his Emergency Banking Relief Act is passed, the first of a string of bills approved by Congress in his first one hundred days in office to help America recover from the Great Depression.

1935

Roosevelt creates the Works Progress Administration and secures passage of the Social Security Act, the most significant piece of New Deal legislation.

1936

On November 3 Roosevelt is reelected president, defeating Alfred Landon.

1941

In March Congress passes the Lend-Lease Act, which provides supplies to nations fighting the Axis Powers; on July 25 Roosevelt embargoes shipments of scrap iron and gasoline to Japan and freezes all Japanese assets in the United States; on December 8 Roosevelt calls the bombing of Pearl Harbor a "date which will live in infamy" and asks Congress to declare war, which it does within hours.

1939

On September 1 German troops invade Poland and begin World War II in Europe.

1943

On January 12 Roosevelt meets with Winston Churchill at the Casablanca Conference, and announces that the Allies will accept nothing less than unconditional surrender from the Axis Powers; on November 28 Roosevelt, Churchill, and Joseph Stalin meet in Tehran, to discuss the upcoming Allied invasion of Western Europe.

1935	1940	1945	1950

1940

On November 5 Roosevelt is elected president for a third term, defeating Wendell L. Willkie.

1942

In February Roosevelt signs an executive order to intern 120,000 Japanese, many of them American citizens; on April 18 bombers take off from the aircraft carrier USS *Hornet* and bomb Tokyo in the first U.S. attack against Japan; on June 6 the United States wins the Battle of Midway; on November 8 U.S. and British soldiers land in Morocco and Algeria to fight the Axis Powers.

1945

In February Roosevelt, Churchill, and Stalin meet at the Yalta Conference to discuss the future of Europe, Asia, and the United Nations; on April 12 Roosevelt dies of a cerebral hemorrhage in Warm Springs, Georgia; on April 15 he is buried at Hyde Park, New York.

1944

In March Roosevelt's physicians express concern about his health; on June 6, D day, the Allies cross the English Channel in Operation Overlord, the greatest military invasion in history; on November 7 Roosevelt is reelected to a fourth term, defeating Thomas E. Dewey.

Franklin D. Roosevelt: Breaking Tradition

As a presidential candidate and then as president, Franklin D. Roosevelt gloried in breaking tradition. The Democratic Party made the New York governor its presidential nominee in the summer of 1932 at its national convention in Chicago. Candidates in the past had waited patiently at home until party officials came to tell them they had been chosen. But Roosevelt defied tradition by not only accepting the nomination in person but flying from Albany, New York, to do it, thus becoming the first presidential candidate to make a campaign trip by airplane.

After a tiring nine-hour flight—air travel was still in its infancy—Roosevelt, his wife, Eleanor, two of their four sons, and members of his staff went to Chicago Stadium. In his acceptance speech on July 2, Roosevelt promised to help tens of millions of Americans suffering in the iron grip of the Great Depression, but he also warned them he would forsake tradition to accomplish that goal:

> I have started out on the tasks that lie ahead by breaking the absurd traditions that the candidate should remain in professed ignorance of what has happened for weeks until he is formally notified of that event many weeks later. You have nominated me and I am here to thank you for the honor. Let it also be symbolic that in doing so I broke traditions. Let it from now on be the task of our Party to break foolish traditions.[1]

Roosevelt held the world's most powerful elected position longer than any other president—twelve years and thirty-nine days, from March 4, 1933, when he was inaugurated for the first of his four terms until his death on April 12, 1945. It is a record tenure that will never be broken; the Twenty-second Amendment to the Constitution, passed in 1951, limits presidents to two terms. In his historic time in office, Roosevelt helped Americans survive the worst economic crisis in the nation's history, led Allied nations to the threshold of victory in World War II, reshaped the office of the presidency for all time, and greatly expanded the scope of federal government operations and the nature of its obligations to its citizens.

Franklin D. Roosevelt, pictured with his wife Eleanor (center) and mother, remains the only person ever elected to four terms as president of the United States.

Roosevelt accomplished this by shattering more traditions than any other president. On the surface, however, Roosevelt seemed an unlikely figure to boldly experiment with the machinery of government and topple the existing status quo.

ROOSEVELT IS SHAPED

The Roosevelts were a rich, powerful family, one whose American roots extended back two centuries. As a person of wealth and privilege, Franklin D. Roosevelt could easily have devoted himself to pursuing a life of ease and luxury. But Roosevelt was strongly influenced by several people—and one catastrophic illness—to become a man who cared deeply about those less fortunate than he was. Reverend Endicott Peabody, who headed the exclusive prep school he attended, and Eleanor Roosevelt, whom he wed in 1905, both fostered in him a deep compassion for the poor and needy. And Theodore Roosevelt, a distant cousin who became president in 1901, provided a heroic role model for government service and ignited Franklin's dream of one day becoming president.

By 1921 Roosevelt had served as a New York state senator and assistant secretary of the navy during World War I and become one of his party's leading national figures. His goal of one day occupying the White House appeared within his grasp. But that August the thirty-nine-year-old Roosevelt was stricken with polio. The illness paralyzed his legs, confining him to a wheelchair and, in the minds of most people, ending his promising political career. After all, how could a "cripple," the demeaning term then applied to those who had disabilities, ever win an election or be strong enough to govern?

But in the next seven years Roosevelt worked hard to regain the use of his legs. His body became heavily muscular in his upper torso from exercise even as his legs withered away. His spirit changed along with his body. Frances Perkins, whom Roosevelt named secretary of labor in 1932, making her the first woman to ever serve in a president's cabinet, once explained Roosevelt's character transformation this way: "There had been a plowing up of his nature. The man emerged completely warm-hearted, with new humility of spirit and a firmer understanding of philosophical concepts."[2]

Laid low by illness, Roosevelt had become more humble and compassionate. In his quest to regain the use of his legs, he had also become willing to try any-

thing to rehabilitate his shattered body. When he was elected New York governor in 1928, he began to apply this new attitude of bold experimentation to the way he governed. On May 22, 1932, Roosevelt, who liked to refer to the states as "forty-eight laboratories for experimentation," outlined this philosophy in a speech at Oglethorpe University:

> The country needs and, unless I mistake its temper, the country demands bold, persistent experimentation. It is common sense to take a method and try it. If it fails, admit it frankly and try another. But above all, try something.[3]

A DANGEROUS TIME

Roosevelt was elected president at one of the most dangerous times in U.S. history. At home, the Great Depression had thrown tens of millions of men and women out of work, creating incalculable hardship and making Americans fearful of the future. Abroad, Germany's Adolf Hitler, Italy's Benito Mussolini, and Japanese militarists were laying the foundations for the savage destruction of World War II.

When Roosevelt took office on March 4, 1933, the world to most Americans appeared to be brutal, bleak, and very frightening. It was Roosevelt, more than any other single person, who would help them survive this dangerous period. Historians Allan Nevins and Henry Steele Commager explain that, somehow, the people and events in Roosevelt's life com-

Roosevelt was stricken with polio in 1921, confining him to wheelchairs and a dependence on canes. He faced this challenge with determination, even seeking experimental therapies to regain use of his legs.

bined to create a president suited to deal with the dire problems facing his nation:

American Democracy has always managed to find great leaders in time of great crisis. In Roosevelt they had a leader who as spokesman for democracy and nationalism was the peer of [Abraham] Lincoln, as a leader towards a better world order the peer of [Woodrow] Wilson.[4]

Chapter

1 Growing Up a Roosevelt

When Franklin D. Roosevelt was attending Harvard University in 1901, he wrote a thesis for a history class about his family, of which he was always inordinately proud. In "The Roosevelts of New Amsterdam," he not only listed his ancestors but tried to explain why they had accomplished so much since arriving in the New World more than two centuries earlier:

> Some of the famous Dutch families in New York have today nothing left but their names—they are few in numbers, they lack progressiveness and a true democratic spirit. One reason—perhaps the chief—of the virility of the Roosevelts is [their] democratic spirit. They have never felt because they were born in a good position they could put their hands in their pockets and succeed. They have felt, rather, that being born in a good position, there was no excuse for them if they did not do their duty by their community.[5]

This youthful bragging was not entirely unwarranted. Through the wealth and political power that members of his family had accumulated since the first Roosevelt arrived from Holland in 1649 to begin a

new life as a humble farmer, they had come as close as any family could to being considered American royalty. Franklin was related by birth or marriage to no less than eleven presidents, including Theodore Roosevelt, a fifth cousin who was leading the nation when he penned those words.

But as much as his family's fame and accomplishments delighted the nineteen-year-old college student, their exalted status was also a heavy burden. Family members repeatedly told him that, as a Roosevelt, he had a duty to live up to his exceptional heritage. "We are proud of our ancestors," an uncle wrote him, "but will our descendants be proud of us?"[6]

EARLY ROOSEVELTS

Franklin was born on January 30, 1882, in Hyde Park, New York, to James and Sara Delano Roosevelt; her family name became Franklin's middle name. His father traced his American roots back to Claes Martenszen van Rosenfelt, who came to the New World from Holland and carved out a farm in New Amsterdam, a Dutch settlement located in what is today Manhattan in New York City. Even as presi-

Roosevelt, pictured here as a child, was proud of his Dutch heritage, later referring to himself as an "old Dutchman."

dent, Roosevelt showed pride in his heritage by referring to himself as an "old Dutchman."

New Amsterdam was a tiny settlement of eight hundred when van Rosenfelt arrived, but by the time of the American Revolution, it had been transformed into a thriving English port of twenty-five thousand known as New York. Like the city in which they lived, Claes's descendants also increased in numbers. As they grew more prosperous, they changed their name; Claes's son, Nicholas, anglicized van Rosenfelt (which in Dutch means "field of roses") to Roosevelt. Two of Nicholas's sons, Jacobus and Johannes, became wealthy from business ventures in real estate, dry goods, and the sugar trade with the West Indies. They also established the two main branches of this distinguished family; Franklin Roosevelt is descended from Jacobus and Theodore Roosevelt from Johannes. The Jacobus line is known as the Hyde Park Roosevelts and Johannes's descendants the Oyster Bay Roosevelts, named after where the most prominent members of the family settled in New York.

The first family member of note was Isaac Roosevelt, the son of Jacobus and Franklin's great-great-great-grandfather, who during the Revolution became known as "Isaac the Patriot." He was a member of a provincial congress that voted for independence, helped create New York state's first constitution, and, with close friend Alexander Hamilton, the first U.S. treasurer, helped win state approval of the U.S. Constitution.

Isaac's son James (the anglicized version of Jacobus) continued to increase the family's wealth, served briefly as a member of the New York State Assembly, and built several homes for his large family— he had three wives and eleven children— including Mount Hope on the Hudson River. His oldest son, Isaac, was born in 1790 and became a doctor. On July 16, 1828, Isaac had a son named James, who was born at Mount Hope and would become Franklin's father.

Pictured here with his parents at Springwood, his parents' large estate, the young Roosevelt lived a life of ease and privilege.

FRANKLIN'S CHILDHOOD

Roosevelt's childhood was one of luxury and ease. During the spring and fall he and his parents lived at Springwood, the family's lavish Hyde Park estate, which encompassed nearly one thousand acres of field and forests along the Hudson River. Even decades later as president Roosevelt would care deeply for Springwood. "All that is in me," he once said, "goes back to the Hudson."[7] The Roosevelts resided in the family townhouse in Manhattan in the winter and toured England and Germany during the summer. James and Sara were loving, attentive parents who lavished af-

fection on their only child, instilling in the young boy a supreme confidence that would be his greatest strength.

Franklin's parents had married four years after the death of James Roosevelt's first wife. Only twenty-six years old, the beautiful Sara Delano Roosevelt was half her new husband's age. One of five daughters of Warren Delano II of Newburgh, New York, who were known in New York society as "the beautiful Delano sisters," Sara was no stranger herself to luxury. The Delanos were also a rich, powerful Hudson River family, and Sara grew into a strong, confident young woman accustomed to always getting her way.

The birth of Franklin, who would be her only child, was a pivotal event in Sara's life. She had a difficult pregnancy and was in labor with Franklin for more than twenty-four hours. Roosevelt biographer Geoffrey C. Ward speculates that the painful, difficult birth heightened Sara's love for her son:

> The hard time may have had much to do with the extraordinarily powerful bond between mother and son that was forged during the first moments of Franklin Roosevelt's life and remained intact until the last instant of hers. "At the very outset [Sara once said] he was plump, pink and nice."[8]

Unlike many wealthy women of the period who let servants care for their children, Sara performed many motherly tasks such as dressing and bathing her son. She also conscientiously oversaw his early education. Until he was fourteen years old, Franklin was schooled at home by tutors in subjects like history, literature, mathematics, French, and German. Like his cousin Theodore, Franklin was a voracious reader, delighting especially in adventure tales and books about the sea. Franklin also became an avid lifelong collector of many things—books and paintings on naval history, birds and animals he shot and stuffed, and stamps.

His passion for stamp collecting was passed on to him by his mother, the single most important influence on Franklin when he was growing up. She strictly scheduled Franklin's daily activities and chose which children he would see; his playmates were all relatives or lived in nearby estates.

Roosevelt was educated at home by tutors until he was fourteen. His friendships and daily activities were strictly monitored by his mother.

However, James Roosevelt, one of Franklin Roosevelt's five sons, believes the influence his grandmother wielded over his father has been exaggerated:

> The contention that Sara completely controlled her son is a fatal flaw in most biographies of my [father]. She may have shaped him some in his youth, as all parents do, but in the end, like most children, he grew up and away from her.[9]

Franklin's father, whom he called "Popsy," also adored his son and spent a great deal of time with him. James took Franklin sledding before he was two and taught him how to ride, row, skate, swim, sail in summer, pilot an iceboat in winter, and shoot and hunt. Franklin pursued such activities at Springwood and at a seaside cottage on Campobello, a slender rockbound island in Canadian waters just off the coast of Maine where the family spent part of each summer. James instilled in his son a love for these two places that never died.

When the Roosevelts traveled outside New York, they rode in a private railroad car, the *Monon*, which had separate bed and sitting rooms and was richly decorated in brass and mahogany. Rail was his father's favorite mode of transportation, and it also became Franklin's; he continued to take long trips by rail as president even though airplanes were faster. By the time Franklin was fifteen he had also visited Europe eight times. Most of the trips abroad were made so that his father, who never fully recovered from a heart attack he suffered in 1890, could visit health spas. In 1891, when his family spent the summer

Roosevelt developed a love of nautical pursuits. He is pictured here on a boat while spending the summer at Campobello.

in Bad Nauheim, Germany, Franklin attended a local school there for six weeks.

GROTON

In the fall of 1896, when Franklin was fourteen, his leisurely, sheltered life came to an abrupt end when he began attending Groton School in Groton, Massachusetts,

CURLS AND SKIRTS AND GUNS FOR FRANKLIN

Unlike many wealthy women of her period, Sara Roosevelt took her duties as a mother very seriously. In FDR: The Beckoning of Destiny, *Kenneth S. Davis explains that she was especially diligent about performing two daily tasks for her son: dressing him and bathing him.*

"Sara was not immune to the [influence of] a best-selling novel of those years, *Little Lord Fauntleroy*, and her son suffered accordingly. Until he was five years old, he wore long curls and dresses [as did the book's hero]. Thereafter his mother dressed him for a time in kilts, complete with a miniature sporran [leather pouch] at his belt and a beribboned Highlander cap. Not until he was nearly eight did he wear pants; he was graduated then to cute little sailor suits. And he was nearly eight and a half when, in a brief letter to his absent father, he proudly announced that, his mother having left that morning, 'I am going to have my bath alone.'—evidently for the first time!

Although the outfits his mother selected for him make young Franklin sound like a sissy to people today, such clothing back then was acceptable for small boys. In any event, Sara did not try to stop her son from masculine pursuits such as hunting, although as Davis reports, she once wrote how angry she was that he began shooting guns at a young age: 'He should never have gotten off to such an early start [shooting and hunting], but already at eleven he had his own gun, given [to] him by his father, and had established a reputation among his playmates for being a crack shot.'"

Franklin and his mother. Sara Roosevelt often dressed her son in elaborate clothing.

a Protestant preparatory school whose students were from other rich, prominent families. Franklin roomed in Hundred House, a spartan dormitory far different from his luxurious home; the entrance to student rooms, for example, was covered by a curtain instead of a door because founder Endicott Peabody believed that young men should not have too much privacy. Students followed a demanding schedule that began with ice-cold showers at 6:45 A.M., a full day of classes and other activities, and ended with evening prayers and a ritual of shaking hands with Peabody.

Franklin was a satisfactory student, but he was less successful in athletics. The tall (nearly six foot), skinny youth struggled in baseball and football, but he fared better in golf and tennis. Although he always reas-

sured his parents in letters that he was fine, Franklin had trouble being accepted by other students. "I always felt entirely out of things,"[10] he once admitted. Part of the problem was that he entered school two years later than other students his age, and they had already formed many friendships; his parents loved him so much they had hated to have him leave home before then. He also seemed different because of his British accent acquired on trips abroad and his overly refined manners.

A polite boy who almost never misbehaved, Franklin wanted to fit in so badly that he deliberately broke school rules. "I have served off my first black mark [punishment for the offense] today, and I am very glad I got it, as I was thought to have no school spirit before,"[11] he boasted in a letter to his parents. Although the offense

TRAVELING CAN BE DANGEROUS

Because his parents were wealthy, Franklin D. Roosevelt traveled a great deal while growing up. His family crossed and recrossed the Atlantic Ocean in trips to Europe, where his father, who had heart trouble, would spend weeks at health spas, bathing in mineral waters that supposedly had healing powers. Roosevelt biographer Ted Morgan explains that one sea voyage in 1885 nearly had fatal consequences for the future president.

"It was a time when crossing the Atlantic was a serious business. There were no covered or enclosed decks. Passengers with cabins [behind] the funnels were powdered with soot. Meals were served at long tables where the plates and glasses fitted [into spaces], and the chairs were screwed to the floors. On the return trip aboard the *Germanic* in April 1885, the ship was tossed in a storm, a bulkhead broke, and water leaked into the Roosevelt cabin. Unafraid, Sara wrapped her fur coat around three-year-old Franklin and said, 'Poor little boy, if he must go down he is going down warm.' After that near-shipwreck, there were no more European trips for a while."

Roosevelt (third row, second from left) attends Groton School, a preparatory school in Massachusetts. His experiences at Groton led to his choice of government service as a career.

was minor, talking in class, he thought it made him more like other students.

Franklin was not always happy at Groton, but the school shaped him in an important way. Peabody preached to his students that they must help those less fortunate and that government service was a good way to do this. "If some Groton boys do not enter political life and do something for our land," he would say, "it won't be because they have not been urged."[12] It was a lesson Franklin took to

heart before he graduated in 1900 and began attending Harvard University.

HARVARD

Harvard proved to be more enjoyable than Groton because Roosevelt had more friends and took part in a host of student activities. The rail-thin Roosevelt, now over six-foot-one but weighing only 146 pounds, continued to pursue sports and

Roosevelt (standing, center) is pictured with Harvard classmates. While at Harvard, he was exposed to progressive ideas about government that would serve as a basis for his political philosophy.

even tried out for the freshman football team. He was quickly cut, however, after being battered about in practice by much bigger, stronger players.

Roosevelt claimed that his greatest Harvard triumph was his election as editor for one semester of the *Harvard Crimson*, the student newspaper he wrote for for several years. His brief flirtation with journalism made him feel a kinship in later years with newspaper reporters, with whom he always had a good relationship.

Although Roosevelt graduated in only three years because some of his Groton courses fulfilled Harvard requirements, he stayed on for a fourth year to do graduate work and serve as *Crimson* editor. The future president never distinguished himself as a Harvard student, and in fact Roosevelt seemed rather bored with his studies. However, his economics and history courses exposed him to new, progressive ideas on government that helped shape his thinking. One emerging theory

Roosevelt acquired was that government should oversee the economy, which was a departure from the accepted rationale that government should allow the nation's economic system to regulate itself.

ELEANOR

At Harvard Roosevelt dated several women, including Frances Dana, whose grandfathers were famed novelist Charles Henry Dana and poet Henry Wadsworth Longfellow. But in 1902 Franklin began spending more and more time with the daughter of the late Elliott Roosevelt, who had been his godfather and was Theodore's brother. Her name was Anna Eleanor Roosevelt, but she was known as Eleanor.

Eleanor was born on October 11, 1884, to Elliott and Anna Hall Roosevelt and was Franklin's fifth cousin once removed. Unlike that of her future husband, Eleanor's childhood was dreadfully unhappy, at times nightmarish and ugly. Her mother died of diphtheria in 1892 when Eleanor was barely eight years old. Her father was an alcoholic and drug addict who squandered his family fortune and died when she was ten. After her mother died, Eleanor and her two brothers lived the next five years in Tivoli, New York, with their grandmother, Mary Livingston Ludlow Hall. Not only was Mrs. Hall a strict old woman who never showed the young girl any affection, but Eleanor was also subjected during this period to the drunken, sometimes bizarre behavior of two uncles who also lived in the big house in Tivoli.

This brief outline of Eleanor's childhood is bad enough, but the details are worse. Her mother, who was very beautiful, constantly told Eleanor she was ugly and mockingly nicknamed her "granny" because she was so quiet and subdued. "She often called me that," Eleanor once wrote, "for I was a solemn child, without beauty and painfully shy and I seemed like a little old woman, entirely lacking in the spontaneity of joy and mirth of youth."[13] The image Eleanor had of herself indicates she was a very sad little girl.

Though she was rejected by her mother, Eleanor loved her father deeply, but he was often absent on drinking binges, especially after he and her mother separated. Eleanor's father loved his daughter very much, as can be seen by a note he sent her on her sixth birthday from Virginia, where he was hospitalized in one of his many futile attempts to quit drinking: "I wish for my Baby Girl the greatest of Joy and the most perfect happiness in her sweet young life."[14] Yet as is common with alcoholic parents, her father often failed the daughter he loved. Once when Eleanor was eight, she and her father were walking with his dogs in New York when he decided to step into the Knickerbocker Club for a drink. He left Eleanor and his pet terriers at the door, and when he failed to return after six hours, the doorman took the sad, frightened young girl home.

Eleanor's father died on August 14, 1893, after a fall following yet another drinking binge. This loss was one of the most painful events of Eleanor's life. When she was fifteen Eleanor finally escaped from her grandmother's unhappy home when she enrolled in Allenswood, a private boarding school for girls near

A Sad, Fearful Little Girl

The contrast between the childhoods led by Franklin and Eleanor Roosevelt is not only stark but tragic. Franklin grew up surrounded by the love and acceptance of two parents who adored him. Eleanor was rejected by a mother who constantly called her ugly and a father who, although he loved her, constantly failed her because of his drinking and drug addiction. In a biography of the couple based on Eleanor's private papers, Joseph P. Lash explains that the lack of love she experienced resulted in a young girl who was afraid of almost everything, from the dark to dogs to other children. Eleanor once admitted that the thing she most feared was "that other people would not like me." The one person the young girl knew who did love her unconditionally was her father, "the one great love of my life as a child," as she once wrote. Even after Elliott Roosevelt died, his memory remained vivid to his daughter, who often fantasized about being with him. In 1927 she wrote about her feelings for her father.

"I knew a child once who adored her father. She was an ugly little thing, keenly conscious of her deficiencies, and her father, the only person who really cared for her, was away much of the time; but he never criticized her or blamed her, instead he wrote her letters and stories, telling her how he dreamed of her growing up and what they would do together in the future. But she must be truthful, loyal, brave, well-educated, or the woman he dreamed of would not be there when the wonderful day came for them to go forth together. The child was full of fears and because of them lying was easy; she had no intellectual stimulus at the time *and yet she made herself as the years went on into a fairly good copy of the picture he had painted."*

Although heartened by her father's love, Eleanor suffered from her mother's rejection and criticism.

Eleanor and Franklin are pictured here at his family's estate in Hyde Park. The insecure Eleanor was surprised at Franklin's interest in her.

London, England. She once said her three years there were the happiest she ever had.

Marriage

Franklin and Eleanor had known each other all their lives, but when they met again in the summer of 1902 after she returned from England, he began to see her in a new light. He had always admired her intelligence, but he now became attracted romantically to the slim, elegant young woman who, despite her mother's abusive comments, was attractive.

It was not unusual for Roosevelts to court their distant cousins, and in the next few months they began to date. Eleanor remembered how Franklin surprised her once by asking her to dance. "He was young and [fun to be with] and good-looking," she said, "and I was shy and awkward and thrilled when he asked me to dance."[15] On November 21 Franklin took her to a college football game; Yale beat Harvard 16-0 despite the future president's vociferous sideline cheering. The next day after attending church and having lunch, they took a walk and he proposed marriage, which shocked the shy, insecure young Eleanor. "Why me? I am plain. I have little to bring you," she said, to which Franklin responded, "With your help, I will amount to something."[16]

Eleanor on her wedding day. Franklin married her in defiance of his mother, who argued that he was too young to marry.

Many people could not understand why Franklin, who because of his wealth and good looks could have married many other women, chose Eleanor. However, despite problems they had during their marriage, Franklin loved her so much he was willing to defy his mother to marry her; Sara believed her son should not marry until he was older and tried to get him to change his mind. The joy he felt at

Eleanor's acceptance is evident in this letter to his mother, in which he argued that the match was a good one:

> Dearest Mama—I am the happiest man just now in the world; likewise the luckiest. And for you, dear Mummy, you know that nothing can ever change what we have always been & always will be to each other—only now you have two children to love & to love you—and Eleanor as you know will always be a daughter to you in every true way.[17]

Always a dominating figure in his life, Sara had become even more important to Franklin when his father died on December 8, 1900. Sara finally relented, and Franklin and Eleanor were married on March 17, 1905, in New York City. Two of the major influences in Franklin's life had important roles in the wedding: Reverend Peabody performed the ceremony, and Theodore, filling in for his deceased brother, gave the bride away.

FRANKLIN AND ELEANOR

The marriage reunited the Hyde Park and Oyster Bay branches of the Roosevelt clan. It also brought together two people who, in their own ways, would shatter tradition and play important roles in the history of their nation for decades to come. Franklin Delano Roosevelt Jr., one of their five sons, claims, "They were a team, and the Roosevelt years, I believe, were more fruitful and creative as a consequence of that partnership."[18]

Chapter

2 Early Success, Then Tragedy

Franklin D. Roosevelt entered Columbia Law School in 1904, but he never graduated. As bored with law courses as he had been with many of his Harvard classes, Roosevelt quit in 1907 after passing the New York Bar exam and began working for the prestigious New York firm of Carter, Ledyard, and Milburn. Married and with one child, Roosevelt settled into a profession that seemed perfectly suited to a person of his intelligence and social standing.

But Roosevelt was not happy in his work. He kept remembering what his cousin Theodore had said during a visit to Groton when Roosevelt was fourteen: "If a man has courage, goodness and brains, no limit can be placed on the greatness of the work he may accomplish. He is the man needed today in politics."[19] Most socially prominent people during that era believed politics was beneath them, and Franklin's father had refused several requests to run for office. But Franklin idolized Theodore and decided to follow in the footsteps of his dynamic cousin, who had been elected vice president in 1900 but became president on September 7, 1901, following the assassination of President William McKinley.

During his first year at the firm, Roosevelt and five other law clerks sat at their rolltop desks and talked about their futures. While his colleagues explained their legal ambitions, Roosevelt candidly admitted he wanted to be president, predicting he would follow the path his cousin Theodore pioneered in reaching the White House by serving first as New York state assemblyman, then assistant secretary of the navy, and then New York governor. "Once you're elected governor of New York," Franklin said, "if you do well enough in that job, you have a good [chance] to be president."[20]

Although the other law clerks believed Roosevelt was simply spinning a grandiose dream, he erred in only one detail of his blueprint for political success. His first campaign was not for the New York State Assembly but the State Senate.

ENTERING POLITICS

Although Oyster Bay Roosevelts were traditionally Republican, the Hyde Park Roosevelts had always been staunch Democrats; the only Republican Franklin ever voted for was Theodore in the 1904 presidential election. Springwood was located in Dutchess County, a Republican stronghold, but in the spring of 1910

As a young man, Roosevelt made his first foray into politics by running on the Democratic ticket for the New York State Senate in 1910.

Democratic Party officials asked Roosevelt to run for the State Senate against Republican incumbent John F. Schlesser. Party officials hoped Roosevelt's famous name could help him win a race no other Democrat could, and he seized this golden opportunity to begin his political career.

Roosevelt's first campaign was tradition shattering. He toured the district in a large red Maxwell with shining brass lamps for headlights, no windshield, and no top. He was the first candidate to campaign by car in New York, and his automobile, an oddity in a time in which most people traveled by horse-drawn vehicles, drew attention wherever he went. Roosevelt also peppered his speeches with sly reminders of his relationship with the president: "I'm not Teddy. A little shaver said to me the other day that he knew I wasn't Teddy. I asked him, 'Why?' and he replied, 'Because you don't show your teeth.'"[21] The reference to his cousin's prominent front teeth always drew laughs from voters while, at the same time, reminding them how influential his family was.

On November 8 the twenty-eight-year-old political newcomer defeated Schlesser 15,708 to 14,568. When his first legislative session began in January 1911 in the state capital, Albany, Roosevelt quickly found himself at the center of a political battle that would bring him fame.

STATE SENATOR

Democrats controlled the New York legislature in 1911, and most individual party members took their orders from Tammany

Hall, the collective term for a group of corrupt New York City politicians. Roosevelt and a handful of fellow Democrats who opposed the powerful Tammany bosses were called insurgents, and their first order of business in the new term was to see to it that New York's next U.S. senator was not Tammany's man, William F. Sheehan, whom they believed had become rich by the illegal use of political influence.

The effort to oppose powerful Tammany Hall made headlines not only in New York but across the country. Roosevelt biographer James MacGregor Burns claims the effort helped boost the freshman senator's budding political career:

[Roosevelt not only] had won national attention, he had strengthened his position in his district, and Progressives

A SENATE EDUCATION

When Franklin Roosevelt was elected to the New York State Senate, he was a political neophyte who knew little about how elected officials got things done. The fight over the appointment of a U.S. senator against Tammany Hall, the powerful New York City Democratic machine that controlled the state party, only began his education into the rough-and-tumble world of politics. Roosevelt quickly came to understand that deciding how to vote on an issue was a complicated process, one that included political factors as well as the merits of an issue, such as who was most qualified to serve in the U.S. Senate. When Democrats opposed Tammany Hall's choice for the Senate, the political machine threatened to oppose bills they wanted passed and to defeat them in the next election. Thus, Roosevelt learned that every vote had its political consequences. In Roosevelt: The Lion and the Fox, *James MacGregor Burns explains this political education.*

"He learned quickly from old Albany hands like [Al] Smith, from newspapermen, lobbyists, and state officials. He mastered [tricks of the] political trade: how to avoid taking a stand on issues and becoming involved in destructive local squabbles, how to deal with local party leaders, how to handle patronage without making an undue number of enemies, how to attract publicity. Above all, he learned the lesson that democratic politicians must learn: that the political battle is not a simple, two-sided contest between opposing parties, or between right and wrong, or between regulars and irregulars, but, as in the [U.S. Senate] episode, a many-sided struggle that moved over broad sectors and touched many interests. A simple farm bill, for example, involved not merely individual farmers but county agricultural societies, canneries, university professors, merchants, railroads, and government officials, and divisions over policy might occur not merely between such groups but within them."

probably remembered his lengthy fight against Tammany long after they forgot the anticlimactic ending. Perhaps more important in the long run, the young politician had been given a telling education in the tactics of pressure and intrigue.[22]

Roosevelt's opposition to Tammany Hall put him squarely in the ranks of Progressives, elected officials from both parties who were trying to pass legislation to help the poor and protect the rights of workers, especially women and children, and to reform government by making it more responsive to citizens. The fight over Sheehan was considered part of the Progressive movement to give people more control over their elected officials. In 1911 U.S. senators in most states were not elected by voters but selected by party bosses who controlled state legislatures.

For three months Roosevelt and others kept up the pressure, ultimately stopping Tammany Hall, a notable achievement. The revolt finally ended when Tammany bosses, realizing they had to compromise with insurgent legislators, switched to a more satisfactory candidate, James A. O'Gorman. The battle taught the young lawmaker a great deal about how politicians worked behind closed doors to influence events, and in time Roosevelt became highly skilled in such maneuvering.

Roosevelt became a popular legislator, not only for standing up to Tammany Hall but for legislation he backed to help constituents in his heavily agricultural district. He drafted and backed bills that allowed farmers to receive low-cost loans and shielded them from being exploited by firms that bought their crops.

Despite his accomplishments, Roosevelt's reelection in 1912 was left in doubt when he was stricken with typhoid fever before the campaign began. Unable to actively seek votes himself, he hired Louis McHenry Howe, a newspaper reporter who was legendary for his political expertise. Howe, who would loyally serve Roosevelt for the rest of his life, wrote newspaper advertisements and a series of letters to voters that were so effective that Roosevelt won without making a single campaign appearance.

NAVY SECRETARY

Roosevelt, however, would not serve a second Senate term. In 1911 he had begun supporting the presidential candidacy of New Jersey governor Woodrow Wilson, the leading Democratic Progressive. When Wilson was elected in 1912, he rewarded Roosevelt by naming him assistant secretary of the navy. Roosevelt desired the position not only because he had immersed himself in naval history and lore since he was a child, but because his cousin had also held that office; after all, Franklin was trying to duplicate Theodore's march to the White House.

As the assistant to Naval Secretary Josephus Daniels, Roosevelt's duties should have been confined to managing details that Daniels assigned him, not making policy or becoming involved in political issues. But Roosevelt, not content with that minor role, used the position to

President Woodrow Wilson (left) selected Roosevelt to serve as an assistant secretary of the navy. Roosevelt was particularly pleased with the appointment because of his interest in naval history.

strengthen his political power. "I get my fingers into everything and there's no law against it,"[23] he said with glee. Although Roosevelt sometimes contradicted statements Daniels made or argued against his policies, Daniels put up with him because Roosevelt was a good administrator. Roosevelt reformed the way navy contracts were awarded, helped lower spending, and became adept at handling labor relations involving almost 100,000 civilian employees.

In 1914 when World War I began in Europe, the nation was divided about what role to play. Most Americans wanted to stay out of the fighting, but some, including Roosevelt, believed America should help the Allied forces of England and France battle Germany and the Austro-Hungarian Empire. Roosevelt strongly advocated "preparedness," a term that meant America should increase its military strength in case it did become involved in the war.

In 1917 when America entered the war, Roosevelt enhanced his reputation as an effective administrator by speeding up construction of ships that were needed to transport supplies to the Allies and helping guide the explosive growth of U.S. naval forces. He was also credited for his innovative idea of floating seventy thousand explosive mines in the North Sea between the northern tip of Scotland and the Norwegian coast to curtail German submarine attacks on Allied ships. The deadly subs were sinking hundreds of ships, and with them the weapons, food, and other supplies they needed to keep fighting.

In the summer of 1918 Roosevelt, who had longed to see the war close up, made an extended tour of naval bases, hospitals, and battlefields in England and France, including Belleau Wood, where U.S. troops a few weeks earlier had stopped a German advance at a cost of thousands of lives. Roosevelt had once asked Wilson for a naval commission (the president turned him down) because, like many young men, he wanted to experience what he thought

---

ROOSEVELT AND WILSON

When Roosevelt became assistant secretary of the navy, it gave him the opportunity to watch President Woodrow Wilson govern the nation. Wilson would have almost as great an impact on shaping the young Roosevelt's attitudes toward how to function as president as his own cousin Theodore did. In Franklin D. Roosevelt: A Rendezvous with Destiny, *Frank Freidel explains the importance of Roosevelt's relationship with Wilson.*

"The move to Washington brought Roosevelt under the influence of Woodrow Wilson, the second of the progressive presidents who made a deep impression upon him. Theodore Roosevelt had been a flamboyant relative, beckoning young Franklin to an exciting life of political strenuosity; Wilson was an austere, revered schoolmaster, like [Endicott] Peabody of Groton, teaching the uses and responsibilities of power. There was never any give-and-take between the president and the youthful assistant secretary, but there were numerous discussions of policy problems. Some of Wilson's remarks made such a lasting impression upon Roosevelt that years later when he himself was in the White House he liked to repeat them. As president, Roosevelt compared TR and Wilson in a way that suggested what he had learned from each of them: 'Theodore Roosevelt lacked Woodrow Wilson's appeal to the fundamental and failed to stir, as Wilson did, the truly profound moral and social convictions. Wilson, on the other hand, failed where Theodore Roosevelt succeeded in stirring people to enthusiasm over specific individual events.'"

Roosevelt tours England in 1918 to witness the war firsthand. He visited naval bases, hospitals, and battlefields in both Britain and France.

was the glory of war. But the visit made Roosevelt realize that war caused so much death and destruction that it was something to be hated, not idealized.

UNHAPPY FAMILY LIFE

Roosevelt returned home from Europe to his own personal battleground—his failing marriage with Eleanor. From the beginning, Eleanor had been unhappy, partly because of Franklin's possessive mother, Sara, who was still trying to control her son's life. When Eleanor and Franklin married they lived in a New York townhouse Sara gave them as a wed-

ding present. The home was furnished with furniture Sara selected and servants she hired, and it was located next door to her own home. It even included a shrine of sorts to her son, a room that featured his collection of stuffed birds, and a three-quarter-length sculpture of young Franklin his mother had commissioned a popular sculptor to create.

Franklin and Eleanor had their first child, Anna, in 1906, and then five sons, one of whom, Franklin Jr., died of pneumonia in November 1909 when he was only eight months old. The sons who survived were James (1907), Elliott (1910), a second Franklin Jr. (1914), and John (1916). Sara, as possessive of her grandchildren as she was of her son, constantly interfered with how they were raised. In the 1930s Eleanor wrote of how bitterly she resented her mother-in-law's meddling:

> She determined to bend the marriage to the way she wanted it to be. What she wanted was to hold on to Franklin and his children; she wanted

them to grow as she wished. As it turned out, Franklin's children were more my mother-in-law's children than they were mine.[24]

Sara also forced Eleanor to quit doing the volunteer work she loved. Eleanor believed deeply in helping those who were less fortunate, and twice a week she rode a public

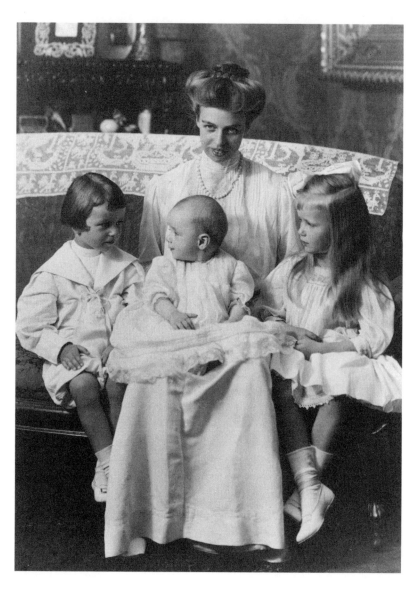

Eleanor is pictured with three of her children, James, Elliott, and Anna (left to right). Her mother-in-law meddled frequently in the upbringing of her grandchildren.

trolley to New York's Lower East Side to teach immigrant youths at the University Settlement House, a private organization that helped the poor, how to adapt to life in America. Giving up the social work saddened Eleanor, but she had never been very happy. Her difficult childhood made her believe she had to rigidly control her emotions and actions, and she once admitted that she had "an almost exaggerated idea of the necessity of keeping all of one's desires under complete subjugation."[25]

Although Franklin loved Eleanor when they married, he was high-spirited and fun loving. He enjoyed socializing with friends, having a few drinks, playing poker, sometimes just acting silly, behavior his somber wife found offensive. The couple had drifted apart emotionally, however, and their physical relationship ended with the birth of their last son in 1916. Roosevelt soon began turning elsewhere for companionship.

A MISTRESS

When Franklin returned from Europe in September 1918 and was stricken with double pneumonia, Eleanor was helping him with his correspondence when she came upon a packet of love letters written to him by Lucy Page Mercer, who had been Eleanor's social secretary since 1913. The letters proved something she had long feared: Her husband was having an affair with another woman.

Franklin enjoyed the company of the beautiful young woman, who was a decade his junior. Trude Lash, a friend of Eleanor's, believes the affair began in 1917 when Eleanor took the children for the summer to Campobello Island, leaving her husband and her secretary behind in Washington. Said Lash, "There was Lucy in the house, and there was lonely Franklin, and I think this developed the way things do develop, with nobody planning them. They just happen."[26]

The discovery of the letters shattered Eleanor and irreparably damaged their marriage. Eleanor offered to divorce him, but Franklin knew that because divorce then was considered immoral, it could ruin him politically. And his mother, fearing a public scandal, threatened to disinherit him if he left Eleanor. Roosevelt agreed to end the affair and stay with Eleanor, but in a biography of his parents, James Roosevelt claims that after the incident there was never any real love between them:

> Father and mother sat down and agreed to go on for the sake of appearances, the children and the future, but as business partners, not as husband and wife. After that, father and mother had an armed truce that endured to the day he died.[27]

The shock of her husband's betrayal forced Eleanor to reassess her life. As she wrote years later, "The bottom dropped out of my own particular world & forced me to face myself, my surroundings, my world, honestly for the first time."[28] Eleanor would eventually emerge from the bitter incident stronger and with more purpose in her life, and through the work she turned to afterward would establish her own unique legacy of accomplishment.

ELEANOR AND FRANKLIN

Although Eleanor and Franklin Roosevelt were married for four decades, their personalities were nothing alike. In Eleanor and Franklin, *author Joseph P. Lash, whose parents were friends of the couple, explains how their differing temperaments created problems in their relationship.*

"Because [Eleanor] could not relax, others found it difficult to be wholly relaxed with her. Duty came first, not fun or pleasure. She still felt awkward at parties, and at dances she put in an appearance and then vanished. While [historian] Arthur Schlesinger, Jr., may have exaggerated when he described Eleanor Roosevelt as 'a woman sternly devoted to plain living, invincibly "sensible" in her taste and dress,' she herself often spoke of the 'Puritan' in her that held her back from high living, frivolity and indolence. Franklin, on the other hand, was debonair, fun-loving, and able to enjoy making a night of it [with his friends]. She knew that she did not satisfy the frivolous, flirtatious side of Franklin's nature."

The Roosevelts had very different temperaments. While Franklin was fun loving and high-spirited, his wife was insecure and serious.

Roosevelt (right) ran for vice president in 1920. He is pictured here with his presidential running mate, James M. Cox.

LOSING AN ELECTION

His marriage in tatters, Roosevelt threw himself into his work and the pursuit of his long-term goal of becoming president. He continued to enhance his reputation as an able administrator, and after America helped the Allies win the war, Roosevelt accompanied President Wilson to France for the diplomatic discussions that resulted in terms for the Versailles treaty, which formally ended World War I.

Roosevelt's growing fame in 1920 helped him win the Democratic Party nomination for vice president alongside presidential candidate James M. Cox, the three-term governor of Ohio. As always, Roosevelt was trying to follow in his famous cousin's footsteps, gloating that he was already four years ahead of Theodore's pace to capture the presidency: "I was delighted. I was only 38, and only one other vice-president had been younger. Theodore Roosevelt had been only 42."[29] During the campaign Franklin constantly referred to his famous cousin, claiming he was Theodore's political heir even though he had been a Republican. The Republicans countered by putting Theodore Roosevelt Jr. on the campaign trail to state flatly that Franklin "does not have the brand of our family."[30]

Americans had gloried briefly in having helped win World War I, but the conflict quickly became unpopular because people mourned the 116,000 U.S. soldiers who died in the fighting and because the nation's postwar economy collapsed. Voters blamed Democrats for this ugly war and on November 2 overwhelmingly elected the Republican ticket headed by Ohio senator Warren G. Harding.

Although the Republicans captured 60.3 percent of the vote, Cox—not Roosevelt—was blamed for the loss. The thirty-eight-year-old Roosevelt, on the other hand, was considered one of his party's brightest young stars.

A Businessman

When the Republicans came to power in 1921, Roosevelt returned to private life. He became a vice president of Fidelity and Deposit Company of Maryland, an investment firm, and in a few years used his political and social connections to double the New York office's business. Roosevelt also became involved in other business ventures in the next decade, some of them successes and some of them failures.

Although Roosevelt threw himself into his new work, he was only biding his time

until 1922 when he expected to run for the U.S. Senate. He continued to be active in politics and in late July 1921 went to Washington to testify before a Senate subcommittee investigating how the Wilson administration had conducted the war. Roosevelt returned to New York tired and exhausted, but forced himself on July 27 to visit a Boy Scout camp at Palisades Interstate Park with other well-known figures. He was president of New York City's Boy Scout Foundation; it was also the kind of thing political figures do for publicity. He was gratified the next day to see his picture in the newspaper, never dreaming that it would become a historic photo: the last ever taken of Roosevelt walking freely and unaided.

Roosevelt then sailed to Campobello Island for a much-needed vacation with his family. Although he did not feel well when he got to his vacation home, the next day he went fishing on the Bay of Fundy. It was a hot day, and Roosevelt was enjoying himself until he accidentally fell overboard into the freezing waters of the Atlantic Ocean. "I'd never felt anything so cold!" he would recall a decade later. "I hardly went under, hardly wet my head . . . but the water was so cold it seemed paralyzing."[31] His friends pulled Roosevelt back on board, but he spent the rest of the afternoon in wet clothes and his muscles ached terribly.

For the next few days Roosevelt continued to feel ill, and when he awoke the morning of August 10 he was even weaker and more drained physically. But it was such a nice day that he took his wife and children sailing. That afternoon after Roosevelt spotted a small brushfire on an island, he and other family members went ashore, beating out the flames with evergreen branches. Back home at Campobello he and the children jogged two miles to a small lake to swim. Later that afternoon Roosevelt even took a dip in the ocean. He usually found the cold waters of the Bay of Fundy exhilarating, but not this time:

> I didn't feel the usual reaction, the glow I'd expected. I sat reading for a while [in his wet bathing suit], too tired even to dress. I'd never felt quite that way before. The next morning [August 11] when I swung out of bed my left leg lagged but I managed to move about and to shave. I tried to persuade myself that the trouble with my leg was muscular, that it would disappear as I used it. But presently it refused to work, and then the other [leg refused].[32]

POLIO

Roosevelt grew sicker that day, and when Eleanor took his temperature and discovered it was 102 degrees, she sent for Dr. E. H. Bennett. Puzzled by the symptoms, the local physician diagnosed it as a cold. When Roosevelt awoke the following day, August 12, he could not stand up, and by nightfall, when he could not move his legs at all, he began to realize his illness was much more serious than a cold. "I don't know what's the matter with me Louis. I just don't know,"[33] he would mutter over and over in the next few days to his aide, Louis Howe.

It would be two more weeks before a Boston doctor would be able to tell Roosevelt what was wrong. He had contracted poliomyelitis, an acute viral infection that attacks the spinal cord and muscles. Roosevelt would be paralyzed from the waist down for the rest of his life. His dream of becoming president seemed as dead as his legs.

3 Overcoming Polio and Making a Political Comeback

When Franklin Delano Roosevelt returned home to the family estate in Hyde Park in late October 1921 after being hospitalized for six weeks, he was still very sick and in constant pain. This active man who loved golf, sailing, and other outdoor activities was paralyzed from the waist down. His upper body and arms were weak, his hands did not work properly, and he could not sit up or even turn himself from side to side. But Roosevelt was adamant from the beginning that "I'm not going to be defeated by a *childish* disease."[34] Although poliomyelitis was known to the public as infantile paralysis because most of its victims were children, it sometimes struck adults as well. After it attacked Roosevelt, he devoted the next seven years of his life to conquering it.

Like his father, James, who visited scores of health spas to strengthen his failing heart, Roosevelt was willing to try anything to regain his mobility. He experimented with massage, saltwater baths, and ultraviolet light; he even allowed therapists to send electric currents racing through his wasted muscles to revive them. He exercised in the water, lifted weights, and every day strapped on heavy metal braces that weighed seven pounds apiece and, with a crutch under each arm, tried to learn to walk again.

But the lurching movement Roosevelt was capable of was only a crude imitation of walking. His hips paralyzed, he could only thrust his crutches in front of himself, one at a time, and then use his upper body to pull his metal-encased legs forward, his feet dragging along the ground. At first he could manage only a few steps. But soon the driveway at Springwood, less than a quarter-mile long, became a symbol of recovery to Roosevelt; if only he could negotiate its entire length, everything would be all right. His daughter, Anna, remembers how horrible it was to watch her father:

I think it's a bit traumatic, when you're 15 years of age and you look up and see your father, whom you have regarded as a wonderful playmate, who took long walks with you, sailed with you, could out-jump you, and do a lot of things, suddenly, you look up and you see him walking on crutches—trying, struggling in heavy steel braces. And you see the sweat pouring down his face, and hear him saying, "I must get down the driveway today—all the way down the driveway."[35]

Roosevelt never made it down the driveway, and when he fell, he would have to lie on the ground writhing in pain until someone came and helped him up. But he overcame polio as much as anyone could, making it a nuisance in his life instead of a handicap so he could pursue his dream of becoming president.

Roosevelt's illness had been misdiagnosed by two doctors, first as a cold and then as a lesion on his spinal cord. It was not until two weeks after he was stricken that Dr. Robert W. Lovett, a specialist from Boston, correctly identified the disease. It is impossible to pinpoint when Roosevelt was exposed to the virus, which invades the body through the respiratory system and takes from three to thirty-five days to incubate. Roosevelt's medical history, however, indicated that he had a weak immune system; at various times as a youth and as an adult, he had suffered from typhoid, throat infections, influenza, double pneumonia, sinus problems, and severe colds.

After being paralyzed, Roosevelt at first attempted to get around on crutches. He eventually resigned himself to using a wheelchair.

The polio virus attacked and killed the nerve cells in his spinal cord, paralyzing him from the waist down and at first almost killing him. Roosevelt's temperature climbed to over 100 degrees, he lost control over lower organs such as his bladder, he was lapsing in and out of consciousness, and he was constantly in terrible pain. The virus made his skin and muscles so sensitive that it was painful for him to be touched at all; even the weight of a bedsheet was excruciating.

Despite still being estranged from Franklin because of his affair with Lucy Mercer, Eleanor cared for him tenderly.

For two nightmarish weeks until Franklin was hospitalized, she slept in his bedroom, bathed him, fed him, and tried to keep his spirits up during the worst days of his life. "I know that he had real fear when he was first taken ill," she admitted, "but he learned to surmount it. After that I never heard him say he was afraid of anything."[36]

Roosevelt was not only afraid but deeply depressed. Raised an Episcopalian, he once admitted that during this time he briefly lost faith in God. He despaired that polio had not only destroyed his physical life, the ability to walk and do other such

LEARNING HOW TO GET AROUND

Once an active outdoorsman and enthusiastic athlete, Franklin Delano Roosevelt now had trouble just standing up. Although he fought hard so that he could regain the ability to walk short distances with the aid of his braces and crutches, Roosevelt was basically confined to a wheelchair the rest of his life. He had to depend on aides to lift him in and out of cars, carry him up flights of stairs, and lug his body into buildings for meetings. But Roosevelt also had to be able to get around on his own when no one was around. The once proud athlete at times had to resort to crawling on the floor of his home or office. Although it would have embarrassed many people to be seen doing something like that, biographer Nathan Miller writes that it was a skill Roosevelt was proud to show off.

"Roosevelt's most harrowing fear was being trapped in a fire, and he learned to crawl down the long halls and the stairways of the house by the strength of his hands and arms. He was proud of this accomplishment and showed no embarrassment in demonstrating it. While dining with . . . Charles Hamlin [and his wife] one evening, he pushed back his chair and said: 'See me get into the next room.' He dropped down on the floor and crawled into the room and pulled himself into another chair. [Mrs. Hamlin, a family friend, said,] 'My husband was so overcome at such courage and seeing that superb young fellow so pleased by being able to do this—that on the plea of hearing the telephone—he went into his den for a while.'"

things, but his political life as well, because he believed that someone who was considered a "cripple" would never be able to win an election. But gradually the supreme self-confidence that was Roosevelt's hallmark began to exert itself, and he decided he would do whatever it took to recover.

FIGHTING POLIO

For the next seven years Roosevelt lived a life curiously divided between business, politics, and recovery. He continued his investment work with Fidelity and Deposit, started a law practice, and pursued private business ventures, some of them not very practical such as a failed attempt to begin blimp service between New York and Chicago. Roosevelt's trusted aide, Louis Howe, kept him up to date on Democratic Party activities while his wife, Eleanor, represented him at political events.

During this period it was Roosevelt's obsessive desire to regain his mobility that occupied most of his time and effort. When Roosevelt left the hospital, his chart noted that he was "not improving." He could sit up by grasping a bar suspended over his bed and swing himself into a wheelchair by using a strap suspended from the ceiling, but he could not stand up. Roosevelt threw himself into rehabilitation, hiring therapists, buying exercise equipment, and traveling extensively to consult with medical experts who might help him.

Roosevelt's single-minded determination to recover awed people. He lifted weights, did strengthening exercises on the floor, and swam for hours. Roosevelt was able to remain upright only by wearing a corset, which straightened his back, and heavy braces that locked into place, immobilizing his dead legs into an erect position. At first he needed two crutches to walk, but eventually he learned to move forward by supporting his weight with two canes or by leaning on another person while using one cane. These crutch-free methods were dangerous. Falling was always a possibility, but Roosevelt employed the canes because he believed they made him look less disabled than crutches did.

The therapy Roosevelt loved the most, and which gave him the best results, was exercising in the mineral-rich waters of Warm Springs, Georgia, a small rural town about eighty miles southwest of Atlanta. He first visited there in October 1924 after hearing that the springs had helped other polio sufferers. The warm (88 degree) waters flowing from Pine Mountain were refreshing and so buoyant that Roosevelt was able to walk and exercise in them unsupported. After just a few days there, he wrote an ecstatic note to Eleanor, who was in New York:

> The legs are really improving a great deal. The walking and general exercising in the water is fine and I have worked out some special exercises also. This is really a discovery of a place and there is no doubt I've got to do it some more.[37]

Roosevelt, as always, was overly optimistic about the progress he was making. He would never regain full use of his legs,

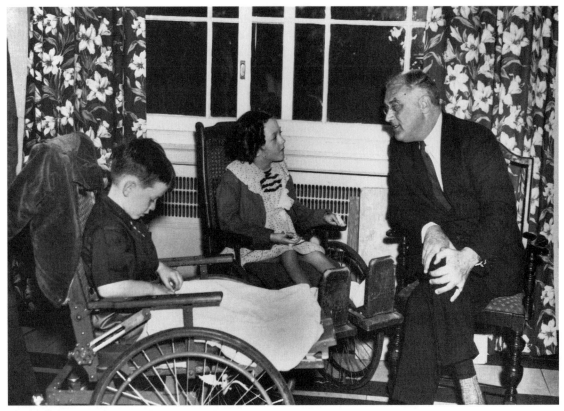

Roosevelt was so impressed with the water therapy he received at Warm Springs that he purchased the town and created the Warm Springs Foundation. Here, he speaks with two disabled youngsters at a Foundation luncheon.

but the water therapy would help him improve his strength, overall health, and mobility. He was so impressed that in 1926 he purchased Warm Springs for $200,000, a sum that was two-thirds of his fortune and today would be valued at more than $1 million, and developed it into the Warm Springs Foundation, a treatment center for polio victims. He served as the director of the center for two years and was an unofficial physical therapist; referred to as "Dr. Roosevelt," he created new exercises and helped people strengthen themselves.

A NEW SPIRIT

During the seven years Roosevelt devoted to beating polio, his slim body changed greatly. Although his legs wasted away, his upper body became full and strong and his weight jumped to 187 pounds, 40 more than he had weighed in college. He boasted that his biceps were bigger than boxing champion Jack Dempsey's, and he liked to arm wrestle with his sons. Polio also transformed his personality. Hugh Gallagher, himself a polio victim confined to a wheelchair, believes the illness reshaped

WARM SPRINGS

One of the happiest moments of Roosevelt's life was the first time he entered the healing waters of Warm Springs, Georgia. Kenneth S. Davis describes this experience in his biography of Roosevelt, FDR: The Beckoning of Destiny, 1882–1928.

"Roosevelt's valet pushed him in his wheelchair to the edge of the pool [and] gently lowered him into the water. At once a 'heavenly warmth' and vitality flowed into his withered legs. 'How marvelous it feels!' he cried out over and over again. 'I don't think I'll ever get out!' Not only the warmth but also the remarkable energizing buoyancy of this highly mineralized water enabled one to remain in it, swimming, floating, exercising for hours on end, without excessive tiredness. On that first morning he remained in for more than an hour. He emerged more refreshed than he remembered having been for years. As Roosevelt wrote that night to [Eleanor,] 'the pool is really wonderful.' Actually, Roosevelt was convinced of a measurable effect during his very first dip; as he stood shoulder-deep in the water, he managed, with concentration, to slightly lift his right foot. His right leg was the stronger of the two—it had been since that ghastly morning at Campobello when he first realized he was becoming paralyzed—but not since the morning of that day had he been able to make it move. He was overjoyed!"

A jaunty Roosevelt is pictured at Warm Springs. He loved the waters there and had been thrilled when, after his first water therapy treatment, he had been able to slightly move his right foot.

Roosevelt. In *FDR's Splendid Deception*, which focuses on how polio affected Roosevelt, Gallagher writes, "I have never met any person for whom the paralysis was not a vital—if not the most vital—shaping event of his life. These polio [survivors] are scarred by their experience as concentration camp survivors are scarred by theirs."[38]

Most biographers agree with Gallagher's contention that polio changed Roosevelt. Before he became ill, Roosevelt was a rich young aristocrat who had always been supremely confident (at times to the point of arrogance), rarely experienced any hardship, and cared little about other people. Afterward, Roosevelt was more patient, humble, serious about life, and compassionate toward others. Eleanor believes polio altered her husband because "Anyone who has gone through great suffering is bound to have a greater sympathy and understanding of the problems of mankind."[39] Howe, who was at Roosevelt's side when he was stricken at Campobello, believes polio affected him this way: "He began to see the other fellow's point of view. He thought of others who were ill and afflicted and in want. He dwelt on many things which had not bothered him much before. Lying there, he grew bigger day by day."[40]

Some historians, however, reject the idea that polio made Roosevelt a different person. James MacGregor Burns, for example, claims that "Roosevelt's illness did not alter but strengthened already existent or latent tendencies in his personality."[41] Kenneth S. Davis believes Roosevelt "was only *somewhat* more serene of spirit, *some-what* more patient and tenacious, *somewhat* more serious, *somewhat* more thoughtful."[42] Burns and Davis, though, seem to be quibbling more about the extent of the transformation rather than whether Roosevelt's illness actually changed him.

Regardless of the extent to which polio affected Roosevelt, his life was not the only one altered by the disease. His wife was greatly affected as well.

ELEANOR CHANGES

When Franklin was struck down by polio, Sara Roosevelt tried once again to exert her will over her son by making him quit politics and live out his life in ease and comfort, as his father had after suffering a heart attack. Eleanor had always lived in the shadow of her domineering mother-in-law, but she and Howe became allies to defeat Sara's attempt to treat her son as an invalid. Although Eleanor once admitted that Sara "dominated me for years," her husband's illness finally "made me stand on my own two feet in regard to my husband's life, my own life, and my children's training."[43]

In fact, Eleanor had already started to create a new life for herself as an independent woman after discovering Franklin's affair. She began making new friends like Marion Dickerman and Nancy Cook, who were active in politics; became involved again in charitable work; and joined civic groups such as the fledgling League of Women Voters. A new phase of her life began when Eleanor represented her ill husband at Democratic Party functions.

FDR's Treatment

Franklin Roosevelt was lucky that he was rich when he got polio. In FDR's Splendid Deception, biographer Hugh Gregory Gallagher explains that when Roosevelt became ill, there was little if any medical help available that average people could afford. Because there was no health insurance, only people who could lay out large sums of money for medical care could make any recovery from catastrophic illness.

"Medical treatment for the handicapped in the 1920s was inadequate, ineffectual, and grim. Most paralytic patients died at the onset of their illness, either from the illness itself [or] from accompanying infection. Patients who did survive [generally] disappeared into the general population. After their discharge from the hospital, most did not seek, nor did they get, any continuing form of rehabilitative therapy."

Gallagher argues that the reason for this lack of care was the negative attitude most Americans had toward people with disabilities.

"In the 1920s, to be handicapped in some visible way carried with it social [stigma]. The handicapped were kept at home, out of sight, in back bedrooms, by families who felt a mixture of embarrassment and shame about their presence. The well-to-do were able to afford custodial nursing care and the loving family was able to care at home for its loved one. Many of the handicapped, however, were simply ignored by their families and society. A New York State study of handicapped children found them to be 'neglected at home, rejected by the schools, incapacitated by physical disability and unable to care for themselves.' There was very little help for such persons."

Even though Eleanor was frightened at first, with Howe's help she began to make speeches and in time became one of the party's most effective female leaders. Working with the new Women's Division of the Democratic Party, Eleanor led a fight to allow women to name their own delegates to the national convention in July 1924. When Franklin praised her for her work, she wrote back with characteristic self-deprecation, "I'm only being active again till you can be again—it isn't such a great desire on my part to serve the world and I'll fall back into habits of sloth quite easily!"[44]

But Eleanor would never surrender the new political role she was creating for herself, just as she would never quit trying to educate her husband about social issues. Those lessons had begun when they started dating and she would ask Franklin to meet her in the slum areas where she was teaching. "My God, I didn't know people lived like that,"[45] Franklin said after one such visit. In the 1920s when she started championing the women's movement and civil rights, she began to influence her husband's views on those issues as well.

POLITICAL COMEBACK

Despite the help of his wife and Howe, Roosevelt was still worried about his political future because he could not walk without the help of braces and crutches, noting to a friend in a letter that "Such a situation is, of course, impossible in a candidate."[46] However, on June 24, 1924, Roosevelt proved himself wrong when he nominated New York governor Alfred E. Smith for president in one of the most dramatic speeches ever given at the Democratic National Convention.

It was not Roosevelt's words that were memorable, but the courage he displayed in making the address despite his paralysis. When it came time to speak, sixteen-year-old James Roosevelt helped his father negotiate the fifteen feet to the podium from his seat in the delegate's section at New York's Madison Square Garden. His sons had all learned how to help their father walk, but it was a difficult process, and James wrote years later, it was never harder than that night:

As we walked—struggled, really—down the aisle to the rear of the platform, he leaned heavily on my arm, gripping me so hard it hurt. I was aware of the silence of the delegates as we worked our way past them. When we got to the rear of the platform, we waited. Father's grip on my arm did not lessen even as we stood there. Then it was time for him to walk alone [to the podium]. He started forward, slowly, looking around to smile at the silent crowd. Step by step, his crutches carried him forward. He did not fall. He reached the rostrum. Leaning forward, he rested one crutch against it and raised one arm to wave at the crowd. He was still smiling. The crowd gave him an ovation.[47]

It was a political triumph. Roosevelt had proven to delegates who had witnessed it and an entire nation that heard his speech on the infant medium of radio that, despite having polio, he was still able to capture their hearts and minds.

WINNING AN ELECTION

Although Roosevelt continued to devote himself to his recovery for the next four years, he remained active in politics and continued to gain the respect of his fellow Democrats. Because of this, Smith in 1928 again asked Roosevelt to nominate him for president. This time Roosevelt went to the podium using only canes, looking extremely fit and once again deeply impressing everyone. Seeing how popular Roosevelt was, Smith pressed him to run for governor in New York to strengthen the Democratic ticket in their home state.

Roosevelt at first refused because he wanted to keep developing Warm Springs and because he was afraid that, if he lost, it would mean the end of his political career. He believed his best chance to win an election would come in a few more years. When Roosevelt finally did agree to run, his opponents immediately questioned whether he was physically able to do the job. Smith deftly deflected the issue, commenting humorously, "A governor does not have to be an acrobat. We do not elect him for his ability to do a double back-flip or a handspring."[48]

Roosevelt further negated the health issue by campaigning hard across the state. He made scores of speeches, as many as seven in one day, often addressing crowds from the back seat of a convertible after locking his braces and pulling himself to a standing position by using a steel rod installed in the back of the automobile. Roosevelt would finish by asking the audience if he looked like a sick man. The crowd, which had witnessed a strong, healthy-looking Roosevelt stand throughout the speech, would laugh at the idea of his being weak or frail.

Roosevelt's association with presidential hopeful Alfred E. Smith (right) led to the rebirth of his own political career. His stirring speech nominating Smith at the Democratic National Convention, convinced the nation that, despite having polio, Roosevelt could still move people's hearts and minds.

Although Smith lost the presidential race to Herbert Hoover, Roosevelt's famous name and eloquence helped him defeat Republican gubernatorial candidate Albert Ottinger, but only by 25,564 votes out of 4.2 million cast. Although the narrow victory led him to jokingly call himself "the one-half of one percent governor,"[49] he had been elected. His comeback was under way.

GOVERNOR ROOSEVELT

In the first of his two terms as governor, Roosevelt pursued an agenda that was in the Progressive mold of his cousin Theodore and Woodrow Wilson. He expanded social services, increased regulatory supervision of business, provided cheaper public utilities for consumers, cut taxes for small farmers, and boosted

---

DRIVING A CAR

The loss of mobility from polio was something Franklin Roosevelt always hated. That is why he was so delighted when he was able to start driving a car again after it was equipped with hand controls he designed. In A First-Class Temperament: The Emergence of Franklin Roosevelt, Geoffrey C. Ward describes how Roosevelt in 1926 bought a battered Model T Ford for $50 and began driving in Warm Springs, Georgia, after a blacksmith installed the controls.

"Franklin wheeled himself out to see his new car, and insisted on going for a drive right away. Just outside of town, Roosevelt took over the car, shuddering jerkily at first as he accustomed himself to the controls, then proceeding smoothly. He was exultant, driving back through Warm Springs at 25 miles an hour, then roaring over to Manchester, then back to Warm Springs again, where he pulled up in front of the drug store, honking his horn and shouting, 'Let's have a Coke!' When the soda jerk emerged with the cold drinks, Franklin was still gleeful. 'How do you like my new car? It's the latest model!' After almost five years of unbroken dependence on others, Franklin was free at last to move about on his own. He couldn't get enough of it, becoming almost as familiar to the people along the dusty roads of Meriwether County as the rural mail carrier. 'Roosevelt drove well,' one frequent passenger wrote: 'his useless feet and legs did not prevent him from controlling the car with the negligent ease of a practiced and confident driver; and we went along steadily enough with frequent stops for short lectures about the countryside.' Thereafter, leisurely drives became a central feature of every visit to Hyde Park, too, and the sight of FDR waving and smiling at the wheel of his blue car became a common one up and down the Hudson."

The resilient Roosevelt in a favorite car. His popularity as governor of New York enabled him to win a second term by an overwhelming margin of votes.

funds for rural education. His programs made him so popular that, in 1930, he was reelected by the overwhelming margin of 725,000 votes.

In 1930, however, Roosevelt was confronted by a much tougher problem. The Great Depression, the worst economic downturn in the nation's history, had started in October 1929 with the collapse of the stock market. By the time Roosevelt began his second term, the U.S. economy had shriveled up, millions of people were out of work, and New Yorkers were looking to Roosevelt for help. Roosevelt responded by creating the New York State Unemployment Relief Act and the Temporary Emergency Relief Administration (TERA), programs that provided financial help to the unemployed. TERA was the first relief agency created in America to combat the depression, and in proposing it Roosevelt argued,

> It is clear to me that it is the duty of those who have benefited by our industrial and economic system to come to the front in such a grave emergency and assist in relieving those who under the same industrial and economic order are the losers and sufferers.[50]

It was a deception that enabled Roosevelt to remain a viable political candidate in a time when disabled people were looked down on. It was a deception that would carry him into the White House, for Roosevelt's landslide reelection victory had made him a leading presidential candidate.

Roosevelt had proved in his first term as governor that he could lead one of the nation's most populous states, and he had displayed a charisma and star quality that made him appealing to people from all walks of life. In the next two years his political advisers and wife, Eleanor, worked tirelessly to build national support for Roosevelt. Their efforts paid off as he fared well in the presidential primaries and caucuses, winning thirty-four states and six territories to hold a commanding lead over rivals like Texas senator John Nance Garner, Louisiana senator Huey Long, and former mentor Alfred E. Smith heading into the 1932 Democratic Convention.

Winning the Nomination

On the first ballot in Chicago Roosevelt received 666 1-2 votes, three times the total for runner-up Smith but 104 short of the two-thirds majority needed. Roosevelt's aides engaged in some political maneuvering, including offering Garner the vice presidency to gain Texas's votes; many hours and several ballots later, Roosevelt was his party's presidential candidate. Roosevelt flew to the convention on July 2

and in his address to delegates to the tune of "Happy Days Are Here Again," his campaign song, Roosevelt coined a phrase that would define his first term:

> I pledge you, I pledge myself, to a New Deal for the American people. Let all of us here assembled constitute ourselves prophets of a new order of competence and of courage. This is more than a political campaign; it is a call to arms. Give me your help, not to win votes alone, but to win in this crusade to restore America to its own greatness.[53]

But before Roosevelt could begin creating the New Deal, he had to defeat the Republican candidate, incumbent president Herbert Hoover. The campaign proved anticlimactic to the convention's tense political infighting as voters rejected Hoover, who had failed to provide significant relief for Americans, and embraced Roosevelt, who promised to help them while delivering speech after speech from the back of his train, the "Roosevelt Special."

President Roosevelt

On November 8 Roosevelt was swept into office with 22,809,638 votes to 15,758,901 for Hoover. His Electoral College victory was even more impressive, 472-59, as Hoover carried only six states. He now faced one of the most difficult tasks that had ever confronted any president—overcoming the Great Depression.

Chapter

4 FDR's First Term: Battling the Great Depression

When Franklin D. Roosevelt took the oath of office on March 4, 1933, as the nation's thirty-second president, America was at the most dangerous point in its history since Abraham Lincoln came to power on the eve of the Civil War, a conflict that almost succeeded in dividing the nation in half. Now in its third year, the Great Depression had created hardship, misery, and suffering throughout the land. One in four Americans, as many as 15 million people, were unemployed, and in big

Roosevelt is sworn in during his presidential inauguration. At this time, the nation was in the third year of the Great Depression.

cities where the jobless rate topped 50 percent, families evicted from their homes slept in tar-paper shacks and scavenged for food in city dumps; eleven thousand of the nation's twenty-five thousand banks had failed, robbing many thousands of depositors of their life savings; business activity had fallen to half its 1929 level; and crop prices were so low that thousands of farmers were losing land that had been in their families for generations.

The United States had survived as a democracy for almost 150 years, but during Senate hearings in January 1933, legislators were stunned to hear how close the nation was to being torn apart. Edward A. O'Neal, an Alabama planter who headed the Farm Bureau Federation, bluntly told one committee, "Unless something is done for the American farmer, we will have revolution in the countryside within less than twelve months." And a few weeks later, Chicago lawyer Donald Richberg warned another legislative body, "There are many signs that if the lawfully constituted leadership does not soon substitute action for words, a new leadership, perhaps unlawfully constituted, will arise and act."[54]

Roosevelt himself realized how dangerous the country's mood was and how much people feared the future. Thus, as Roosevelt drafted the words that would make up his historic first inaugural address, he realized that his most important task was to reassure Americans that everything would be all right. Seconds into the speech, Roosevelt did just that:

This great Nation will endure as it has endured, will revive and will prosper.

So, first of all, let me assert my firm belief that the only thing we have to fear is fear itself—nameless, unreasoning, unjustified terror which paralyzes needed efforts to convert retreat into advance.[55]

The eloquently simple phrase "the only thing we have to fear is fear itself" is one of the most famous ever spoken by a president. It was exactly what Roosevelt needed to say that day. His words soothed the fears Americans had for the future by giving them hope that the federal government would finally help them, which is what Roosevelt had promised during the presidential campaign.

THE GREAT DEPRESSION

When Herbert Hoover took office in 1929, he had proudly proclaimed, "We in America are nearer to the final triumph over poverty than ever before in the history of any land."[56] Yet in his first year as president, his vain boast withered away as the economy died. The United States had gone through at least seventeen economic downturns in the past; called "panics" or "depressions," they were considered a natural part of recurring economic cycles. But none had ever been as severe or as long as the one that is dated from the collapse of the stock market in October 1929 and that eventually became known as the Great Depression.

Historians even today do not fully understand what caused this massive financial failure. Although the economy had been slowing down for more than a year,

THE GREAT DEPRESSION

It is difficult today to imagine the fear and misery the Great Depression caused. But in From the Crash to the Blitz: 1929–1939, *author Cabell Phillips tries to explain how desperate people were when Franklin Delano Roosevelt became president.*

"No New Year ever dawned with less hope than 1933. The Great Depression, having grown progressively worse for three long years, had spread a pall of fear and desperation across the whole land. The physical signs of distress were everywhere. You encountered them with wearying monotony every day: clusters of hungry men and women waiting like docile peasants for food handouts at the relief stations; the smokeless chimneys and rusting sheds of factories standing mute and empty behind their locked gates; the abandoned shops and stores; the drooping shoulders of a father, husband, brother, or friend whose pride had been battered into lethargy and dejection by months of fruitless job hunting. But even worse than this physical evidence of breakdown was the knowledge that it was everywhere—not just in your town or your state or your part of the country. The blight spread across the whole nation—big cities, small towns, the limitless countryside—like a deadly plague of the Middle Ages. Nor were its victims just certain kinds of people. They were farmers, bankers, carpenters, lawyers, factory workers, preachers, chorus girls. But even those who still had jobs or income lived with a hot ball of fear in their stomachs that tomorrow their luck would run out. 'What will I do then?' sprang equally from the tortured clerk behind the counter and the merchant behind his desk."

with some factories closing and farmers struggling because of low crop prices, the nation seemed prosperous. The economy had grown dramatically since the end of World War I, with stock market profits a key factor in driving this economic surge. But in October when investors tried to sell off huge chunks of stock and there were few buyers, prices began to fall, and within a month the value of stocks listed on the New York Stock Exchange dropped 40 percent to $26 billion. Although the stock market crash did not directly cause the Great Depression, it played a huge role in the economic downturn. Historian Robert Kelley explains:

The stock market crash suddenly wiped away enormous stores of capital, and in time the entire economy was made shakier, for it was now less able to be fed by a steady flow of

A woman living in a primitive shack tries to eke out a living by taking in washing and ironing. People everywhere were having difficulty trying to make ends meet.

investment. The stock market crash also had a profound psychological impact. It pricked the bubble of belief in ever-expanding prosperity, drained away confidence in the stockbrokers and bankers who had been leading the speculation, and led ordinary citizens to withdraw their money from investments and hold it as cash.[57]

The collapse ignited a downward economic spiral in prices, production, employment, and foreign trade that caused factories to close, businesses to fail, and banks to fold. The world economy, already weak because many nations were still struggling to rebuild from the devastation of World War I, also slowed down, intensifying U.S. financial problems. By mid-1932 more than 13 million Americans were unemployed, and even those who still had jobs were earning less because wages had fallen drastically. Americans, however, were not concerned with what caused the economic disaster; they only wanted to know what the government was planning to do to end the crisis and help them.

GOVERNING PHILOSOPHIES

Hoover was not willing to do much because Republicans believed the federal government should not interfere with the economy or regulate how business and industry operated. President Calvin Coolidge, under whom Hoover served as secretary of commerce, once proclaimed, "The chief business of the American people is business."[58] So it was only natural that Hoover would comment in November 1929 that "any lack of confidence in the basic strength of business is foolish"[59] and that he would continue to have faith that the business community could overcome the economic problem on its own.

Hoover's reluctance to involve the federal government was evident as late as January 1932 when he criticized a bill that would have granted states $500 million for relief and public welfare. Partly because of Hoover's opposition, the measures were rejected even though many people were hungry, homeless, and desperately needed help. Americans were so angry with Hoover that, during an appearance in Detroit during the 1932 presidential campaign, some people shouted, "Hang him! Hang him!"

Roosevelt was willing to act because he had a completely different view of government. "This contest," Roosevelt said in his last speech of the campaign, "is more than a contest between two men. It is

The unemployment during the depression was staggering. The idle and despondent men pictured here desperately need jobs, but none were found.

more than a contest between two parties. It is a contest between two philosophies of government."[60] Roosevelt had defined his philosophy of how government should act in a message to the New York legislature in August 1931 when he requested relief for jobless workers:

What is the state? It is the duly constituted representative of an organized society of human beings—created by them for their mutual protection and well being. The state or the government is but the machinery through which such mutual aid and protection is achieved. Our government is not the master but the creature of the people. The duty of the state towards the citizens is the duty of the servant to its master.[61]

ASSASSINATION ATTEMPT

In the long period between his election as president and his inauguration, Franklin Delano Roosevelt traveled to many parts of the nation. On a stop in Miami on February 15, 1933, he was almost shot to death by Giuseppe Zangara, an unemployed bricklayer from Paterson, New Jersey, who claimed, "I hate all presidents." While Roosevelt was sitting in an automobile and talking to Chicago mayor Anton Cermak after addressing some ten thousand people at Bay Front Park, Zangara fired six times at the president-elect. Roosevelt was not hit, but Cermak was struck twice and died and four other people were wounded. In Franklin D. Roosevelt: Launching the New Deal, *Frank Freidel quotes the account Roosevelt gave to reporters the next day.*

"I heard what I thought was a firecracker, then several more. I looked around and saw Mayor Cermak doubled over and [a woman] collapsing. I motioned to have [Cermak] put in the back of [his car]. The trip to the hospital seemed thirty miles long. I talked to Mayor Cermak nearly all the way. I remember I said, 'Tony, keep quiet—don't move. It won't hurt you if you keep quiet.' The police did one quick and clever thing. When they got [Zangara] up from the ground they saw [a] car two cars behind mine. They threw the man [Zangara] on the trunk rack and three policemen sat on him."

Freidel writes that Raymond Moley, one of the president-elect's aides, was deeply impressed that Roosevelt never got scared, even hours afterward.

"There was nothing—not so much as the twitching of a muscle, the mopping of a brow, or even the hint of a false gaiety—to indicate it was any other evening in any other place. Roosevelt was simply himself—easy, confident, poised, to all appearances unmoved."

After his victory in the 1932 presidential election, Roosevelt had to wait almost four months before beginning his term. The incumbent president, Herbert Hoover (pictured), took little action during this time period to deal with the depression.

TAKING CHARGE

After winning the election in 1932, Roosevelt had to wait nearly four months to start putting his philosophy into action, for the Twentieth Amendment to the Constitution, which moved the start of the presidential term from March 4 to January 20, would not take effect until 1936. During the long period in which Hoover was president in title only, the economic situation worsened and the banking system failed almost completely. In his inaugural speech Roosevelt said he would fulfill the demand of Americans for "action, and action now" by immediately proposing leg-

islation. He also warned that if Congress failed to pass his programs or to enact reasonable substitutes, he would take even more drastic measures:

> [In] the event that the national emergency is still critical, I shall not evade the clear course of duty that will then confront me. I shall ask the Congress for the one remaining instrument to meet the crisis—broad Executive power to wage a war against the emergency, as great as the power that would be given to me if we were in fact invaded by a foreign foe.[62]

Roosevelt remembered the unlimited power Woodrow Wilson wielded during World War I, when Congress gave him control of the economy and the right to regulate how people lived, from rationing food to censoring news. Roosevelt was warning Congress now that if it did not go along with his plans, he might seek similar powers to confront the problem. The president, however, never had to do this. Congress was so shaken by the menace of the depression that it became a willing partner in not only fighting its effects but transforming forever the very nature and scope of federal government.

The speed with which Roosevelt took control can be seen by how swiftly he acted on the banking crisis. The day after his inauguration, on Sunday, March 5, Roosevelt issued two proclamations—one calling Congress into special session on March 9 and the other declaring a four-day bank holiday.

When Congress convened on March 9, Roosevelt presented it with the Emergency

Banking Act. The bill was read in the House at 1:00 P.M., and representatives passed it on a unanimous voice vote after only thirty-eight minutes of debate, even though many were not sure exactly what it said because there was only one copy of the bill. The act was also approved quickly in the Senate with little debate and only seven "no" votes. Roosevelt signed the bill into law that night at 8:36 P.M.

The unbelievable speed with which the bill passed was a stunning display of the new president's ability to inspire Congress to approve his agenda. The act empowered federal bank investigators to review the nation's existing financial institutions to determine which were strong enough to survive. It also authorized massive infusions of cash into qualifying banks, enabling them to reopen on March 13. "Capitalism was saved in eight days,"[63] proclaimed presidential aide Raymond Moley. Moley was guilty of hyperbole, but reopening the banks helped restore confidence in the economy and calm the fears Americans had about the future.

The bank bill was just the first of a flood of measures that Roosevelt would propose and Congress would pass in the next three months to provide relief, put people to work, and reform business practices to prevent future economic problems. Collectively, these measures would be known as the New Deal.

THE NEW DEAL

Although Roosevelt was an innovator and a tradition breaker, he always under-stood that not every new idea would work. "I have no expectation," he once admitted in a sports-minded reference to baseball, "of making a hit every time I come to bat. What I seek is the highest possible batting average."[64] But in Roosevelt's first one hundred days in office— a period in which he was so effective in winning acceptance of his programs that that time span would become a traditional measuring stick of every new president's success in assuming leadership of the nation—he made a hit almost every time he stepped to the plate.

Roosevelt established the Federal Emergency Relief Administration (FERA), which granted $500 million to state agencies for direct relief. He also created the Civilian Conservation Corps (CCC), a program that at its peak employed a half-million young men in reforestation and flood control work, and the Civil Works Administration (CWA), which by the end of 1933 had employed 4 million people. The Reconstruction Finance Corporation (RFC), which Hoover had established, became the New Deal's key loan agency, making loans to small and large businesses and providing mortgage relief to millions of farmers and homeowners in danger of losing their property.

To make sure farmers got a fair price for crops, Roosevelt created the Agricultural Adjustment Administration (AAA), which dispensed crop subsidies. He also proposed the National Industrial Recovery Act (NIRA), which included an appropriation of $3.3 billion for public works, and the Tennessee Valley Authority (TVA), a huge federal project that created jobs and

A Different Kind of First Lady

The nation had never seen a first lady like Eleanor Roosevelt. Not content to meekly tend the White House while Franklin was running the nation, she became the first activist wife of a president. In The Glory and the Dream, *historian William Manchester paints a portrait of her whirlwind activities.*

"The President could seldom tour the country, so his First Lady covered forty thousand miles every year, delivering lectures and visiting slums, nursery schools, playgrounds, sharecroppers. Franklin always questioned her closely when she returned; he gave her the Secret Service code name Rover. 'For gosh sakes,' said one goggle-eyed miner to another in a *New Yorker* cartoon, 'here comes Mrs. Roosevelt!' In Washington, Eleanor held a press conference once a week for women reporters. Her column, *My Day*, appeared in 155 newspapers. She wrote a question-and-answer page for each issue of the [monthly magazine] *Women's Home Companion* [and had] twice-a-week radio broadcasts. To her admirers she was mother, wife, politician, stateswoman, journalist, and First Lady—all at once, and often all at the same time. She broke more precedents than her husband, had a greater passion for the underdog, and was always a little further to the left. Her critics called her a busybody, a do-gooder, a bleeding heart. Once she wondered whether her outspokenness might be a liability to Franklin. (At the time she was defending the right of Americans to be Communists.) He chuckled and said, 'Lady, it's a free country.'"

Eleanor rewrote the role of First Lady, taking a much more active approach than those who preceded her. She had both admirers and critics, but her husband approved of her activities.

The president talks with farmers. He created the Agricultural Adjustment Administration—one of many aid programs—which subsidized the prices farmers received for their crops.

helped impoverished southern states by providing flood control, cheap hydroelectric power, and regional planning.

Roosevelt also created agencies to regulate business and industry. The Public Utility Holding Company Act coordinated public utilities; the Securities and Exchange Commission (SEC) regulated stock market operations and established rules for securities trading that safeguarded investors; and the Federal Deposit Insurance Corporation (FDIC) regulated commercial banks and guaranteed that depositors would never again lose all their savings if an insured bank folded. Roosevelt also helped the growing labor movement by supporting the National Labor Relations Act, which strengthened the right of unions to bargain with employers, and created a National Labor Relations Board (NLRB) to review labor disputes.

The president also curbed government spending, a major campaign promise. The second piece of legislation he sent to Congress on March 10 proposed major budget cuts, including reducing federal workers' salaries by $100 million and military veterans' benefits by $400 million. Despite the outrage of the powerful veterans lobby, his proposal passed easily.

THE SECOND NEW DEAL

Although the programs Roosevelt created in his triumphal first one hundred days had begun to improve conditions, he realized in 1935 that more needed to be done. Outright panic had disappeared and the downward economic spiral was over, but 10 million people were still unemployed and many people still needed help. So Roosevelt authorized new bills that would have a huge impact on the nation not only then but in the future.

Approved in 1935, the massive Works Progress Administration (WPA) in the next six years would spend more than $11 billion on some 250,000 construction projects, including twenty-five hundred hospitals and fifty-nine hundred schools. The $5 billion initially granted the WPA was the largest single appropriation in U.S. history at that time. Roosevelt also established the Rural Electrification Administration (REA), which helped bring electricity to rural areas across the country, reshaping the way people lived perhaps more than any other New Deal program. In addition Roosevelt won passage of the Revenue Act of 1935, which was branded the "soak the rich" tax plan because it hiked taxes in the upper brackets from 59 percent to 75 percent and increased corporate taxes.

In 1935 Roosevelt also proposed—and Congress passed—the Social Security Act, which created a federal-state program of pensions for senior citizens paid for by a tax on employers and employees; workmen's compensation for jobless workers; and benefits for blind and other disabled people. At that time the United States was the only industrial nation in the world without national old age and unemployment insurance. Although Social Security

was attacked as un-American and opponents claimed it would take away the incentive people had to work, it passed, just as all of Roosevelt's major proposals did. Today Social Security is the single most important guarantee people have that they will have some retirement income when they become too old to work, regardless of how much or how little they manage to personally save.

PERSONAL STYLE

One of the main reasons Congress kept passing the bills Roosevelt proposed was that he was extremely popular. He had won the respect and affection of Americans during the campaign and in his inaugural speech, which people across the nation listened to on radio. Realizing the power of this new medium, Roosevelt began using radio to generate public support for his programs. One of the most unique ways he did this was through his "fireside chats," simple broadcast talks that boosted his popularity and won support for his programs.

His first chat was on March 12, 1933, a day before the banks reopened. Roosevelt wanted to reassure citizens it would be safe to use banks again. In simple terms the president explained how these financial institutions worked and what the government had done to make them more stable, saying, "I can assure you that it is safer to keep your money in a reopened bank than under the mattress [something many people were doing because they did not trust banks]."[65]

FIRESIDE CHATS

Franklin Delano Roosevelt was an innovator, so it was no surprise when he began using the new medium of radio more effectively than any political figure ever had. Pulitzer Prize-winning historian Doris Kearns Goodwin, who has written extensively about Roosevelt, once discussed the power of his fireside chats in a lecture at Kansas State University.

"I always assumed that he was on the radio every week as our presidents currently are, only to discover that he only delivered two or three of these fireside chats every year, deliberately holding himself back to wait for the moment when the country needed to hear from their president. He understood something that modern politicians seem not to have understood, that less is more. That if you hold yourself back and go forward when you are needed, the country will mobilize around your thoughts. [After one speech,] telegrams came in to the White House urging him to go on the radio every day. They said the only way morale [during World War II] would be sustained would be if you talked to us every day. But he wrote back, showing insight, to one of his writers saying, 'If my speeches ever become routine, they will lose their effectiveness.' What [Roosevelt] understood was something that Saul Bellow, the novelist, also understood. In his memoirs he talked about listening to Roosevelt's fireside chats and then while walking down the street on a hot Chicago night in the summer, he said everybody, if you looked in the windows, is listening in their kitchens and their living rooms, and you could keep walking down the street and not miss a word of what Roosevelt was saying because the whole country was tuned in. Bellow said what was important was not simply Roosevelt's voice, but the awareness listening to him that everyone else was sitting in their kitchens and parlors listening to him, too. Which meant you felt connected to your fellow Americans. And when a leader is able to make us feel connected to one another, that is the most important power that they can generate. And Roosevelt certainly did that, that was part of the magic of his leadership."

Roosevelt found the radio to be a powerful communication tool. The broadcasts of his fireside chats educated the public concerning important issues and added to his popularity.

People were amazed, almost flattered, that a president would talk to them directly on such an important subject. The power of Roosevelt's chat was evident the next day when bank deposits exceeded withdrawals in every city, even though the reverse had been expected because people had not been able to access their accounts for several days. Within a week three-fourths of the nation's banks were again doing business.

FDR's Vision

Of all the New Deal programs, perhaps none had a greater long-term effect on American life than Social Security. Its creation marked the beginning of what became known as the welfare state, the federal and state government policies that guaranteed assistance for the poor, the disabled, and others in times of need. Roosevelt once explained to Labor Secretary Frances Perkins the vision he had for the future of such programs:

> There is no reason why everybody in the United States should not be covered. I see no reason why every child, from the day he is born, shouldn't be a member of the social security system. When he begins to grow up, he should know he will have old-age benefits direct from the insurance system to which he will belong all his life. If he is out of work, he gets a benefit. If he is sick or crippled, he gets a benefit. Cradle to the grave—from the cradle to the grave they ought to be in a social insurance system.[66]

Just as he had once wanted to heal patients at Warm Springs, earning him the honorary title "Dr. Roosevelt," he now wanted to help all Americans. Roosevelt's vision of social protection, which was at the heart of the New Deal, now earned him another title, "Dr. New Deal."

5 FDR's Second Term: Battling His Enemies

In 1936 Franklin Delano Roosevelt was the most beloved man in America. He was also the most hated. However, the fact that many more people revered Roosevelt than despised him was evident: He won a second term in the most one-sided presidential election in U.S. history.

The reason for Roosevelt's stunning success was that his New Deal had begun to help the nation recover from the Great Depression. In his first four years, 6 million jobs were created, national income rose 50 percent, factory production almost doubled, farm income nearly quadrupled, and corporations, which in 1932 had lost $2 billion, recorded 1936 profits of $5 billion. Even though nearly 8 million people were still unemployed, conditions had improved and people were feeling better about the future, like this woman, whose husband was working again thanks to a new federal program: "We aren't on relief any more," she could say with pride, "my husband is working for the government."[67]

Roosevelt himself admitted, "There's one issue in this campaign. It's myself, and people must be either for me or against me."[68] But despite the fact that in 1936 almost two-thirds of Americans voted for him because they welcomed the new role government played in their lives by providing jobs and helping to feed and clothe their families, Roosevelt had many powerful enemies who were convinced he was destroying the nation's democratic heritage.

This animosity toward Roosevelt was more intense, bitter, and irrational than that directed against any president in history, with the possible exception of Abraham Lincoln. Many of Roosevelt's critics hated him so much that they refused to use his name, referring to him in private only as "that man" or even "that madman" in the White House.

ROOSEVELT'S VICTORY

Roosevelt's opponents in 1936 had wanted not only to defeat him but to undermine his New Deal. So in accepting his party's presidential nomination before an estimated 100,000 people on June 27 at Franklin Field in Philadelphia, Roosevelt had openly criticized the individuals, corporate leaders, and other political conservatives who were his foes: "These economic royalists complain that we seek to overthrow the institutions of America. What they really complain of is that we seek to take away their power."[69]

Those words were greeted by thunderous ovations from a Democratic Party more strongly unified than ever before by New Deal programs that had helped them. Southerners, union workers in big cities, farmers, African Americans, and liberals banded together in the Roosevelt Coalition, an alliance of seemingly disparate groups that would help the Democrats become the nation's majority party for the next four decades. Democrats fanned out from Philadelphia after Roosevelt's

---

FALLING IN PHILADELPHIA

It was always dangerous for Franklin Roosevelt to walk aided only by canes, but he often did this in public to make his disability look less severe. And on June 27, 1936, when he accepted the Democratic Party presidential nomination at Franklin Field in Philadelphia, his attempt to conceal the extent of his disability almost ended in disaster. While walking to the podium using two canes and leaning on his son Jimmy for additional support, Roosevelt stopped to shake hands with poet Edwin Markham. The president's body shifted, the knee-lock on his left leg braces snapped open, and he began to fall. His bodyguard, Gus Generich, and Secret Service agent Mike Reilly moved quickly to catch him. Since Roosevelt could not stand alone until the brace was fixed, his staff surrounded him so the crowd would not see how helpless the president was. The next day Roosevelt talked to reporters about what had happened, but they never made the story public until years later. The following account is from Geoffrey C. Ward's A First-Class Temperament: The Emergence of Franklin Roosevelt.

"There I was hanging in the air, like a goose about to be plucked, but I kept on waving and smiling, and smiling and waving. I called to Jimmy out of the corner of my mouth to fix the pin. 'Dad,' Jimmy called up, 'I'm trying to pick up the speech.' 'To hell with the speech,' I said. 'Fix the brace. If it can't be fixed there won't be any speech.' But I didn't lose a smile or a wave [to the crowd]. By this time I was mad clear through. First I was mad because Jack Garner [the vice president who had introduced him] had mangled my name, calling me 'Delaney.' I was mad at the speech which scattered on the floor. Finally, and above all, I was mad at the brace which had picked that moment of all moments to break down. I could feel Jimmy fumbling [with the brace] and then I heard the pin snap back into place. My balance was restored and the weight was lifted from poor Gus [Generich]. Jimmy shuffled the pages into proper order, but with some difficulty because he was flustered. [Roosevelt then mounted the podium and gave the speech.]"

stirring speech to work to send him back to the White House, and Republican nominee Alfred M. Landon never had a chance.

In a whirlwind campaign Roosevelt had given scores of speeches, usually greeting voters by saying gleefully, "You look happier than you did four years ago!"[70] In his last speech of the campaign, Roosevelt, realizing he was going to win big, mentioned his political enemies again in a voice full of emotion: "Never before in all our history have these forces been so united against one candidate as they stand today. They are unanimous in their hatred for me—and I welcome their hatred."[71]

And on November 3, 1936, Roosevelt overwhelmed Landon 27.7 million to 16.6 million votes, the biggest popular plurality ever. His Electoral College win was astounding: 523-8. Landon, who was governor of Kansas, had not even carried his own state, winning only in Maine and Vermont.

OPPOSING THE NEW DEAL

Despite his overwhelming victory in his second race for the presidency, Roosevelt was hated by some segments of society. His enemies were mainly the rich—who

Franklin and Eleanor in high spirits on the campaign trail. Although Roosevelt had many detractors, he was an extremely popular president and won the election to a second term by a landslide.

THE IMPORTANCE OF THE NEW DEAL

The New Deal programs Roosevelt introduced in his first two terms were impressive in their innovation, massive in scope, and profound in the way they affected the nation. However, Roosevelt biographer Nathan Miller claims that the most important effect of the New Deal was that it changed the basic philosophical foundation of how the nation would be governed in the future.

"Although [the New Deal] marked the zenith of reform in the United States and produced profound changes in American institutions, with a continuing impact [today], debate still rages over its place in the American political tradition. It altered for all time the relationship between Americans and their government. One of the few successful gradualist revolutions in history, the New Deal centralized power in the national government, and in the hands of the President in particular. The United States was transformed from a nation of individualists into a social-minded community that accepted the principle of the welfare state and the planned society. For the first time, the goal of government became a better way of life for all Americans—and nothing was out of bounds. Innovator and conservator, Roosevelt dealt the American people a new hand, but he used the old deck of cards. 'The New Deal [Roosevelt said in 1934] seeks to cement our society, rich and poor, manual workers and brain workers, into a voluntary brotherhood of free men standing together striving for the common good of all.'"

labeled Roosevelt, himself descended from a wealthy family, a "traitor to his class" because he had increased their taxes—and business and industry leaders who believed he had been wrong to vastly increase the power of federal government and extend its presence into so many new areas, especially regulation of their companies. His cousin Theodore had angered the same powerful political forces during his presidency by working to break up giant businesses called trusts that had become so powerful they were gaining control of the U.S. economy.

Even as Congress was approving his New Deal legislation in the first few months of his presidency, Roosevelt's opponents had begun to attack him. In late June 1933, Republican senator Henry D. Hatfield of West Virginia had denounced the New Deal:

This is despotism. This is tyranny. This is the annihilation of liberty. The ordinary American is thus reduced to the status of a robot. The president has not merely signed the death warrant of capitalism, but has ordained the mutilation of the Constitution unless the friends of liberty, regardless of party, band themselves together to regain their lost freedom.[72]

Because Democrats controlled both houses of Congress, Republicans and others who opposed the president and everything he stood for had initiated a number of legal challenges that claimed that New Deal programs were unconstitutional. When the lawsuits were finally heard by the U.S. Supreme Court, many New Deal programs were overturned. The defeats were partly because most of the justices were conservatives who opposed Roosevelt's political philosophy. In addition, however, some of the programs were not working very well because the hastily drafted enabling legislation had been flawed.

The first big judicial setback came on May 27, 1935, a day New Dealers labeled

---

THE ROOSEVELT COALITION

In the 1936 presidential election, the elements that would make the Democratic Party the nation's dominant party for the next half-century came together in what became known as the Roosevelt Coalition. In From the Crash to the Blitz: 1929–1939, *historian Cabell Phillips explains that this unique political mixture started with the party's traditional base, southern states and big cities in eastern and a few midwestern states. The New Deal policies of Franklin Delano Roosevelt rounded out this new coalition by bringing in union workers, African Americans, and members of the academic and intellectual community, who were liberal in their views.*

"It was in the 1936 campaign that the so-called Roosevelt Coalition first displayed its formidable might. It transformed the Democratic Party from a loose confederation of feuding chiefdoms into a cohesive popular front that would dominate the political stage [for decades]. The Democrats had been an ineffectual minority, nationally at least. But after 1936 the Democratic Party was unmistakably the majority party. It chose the occupant of the White House for all but eight of the next thirty-two years and had effective control of all but three Congresses from the seventy-fifth through the ninety-first. Though it seethed constantly like a houseful of incompatible cousins and in-laws, it was a union of convenience and necessity. In the clinches, all the factions realized there was more to be gained by sticking together than by flying apart. The Roosevelt Coalition altered the design of the Democratic Party and it made issues—ideology—its driving force. In the Roosevelt Coalition, class interest and ideological aims displaced the old narrow parochialism of partisan identification. It transformed the Democratic Party into a truly national party."

"Black Monday" because the Supreme Court declared the National Recovery Administration (NRA) unconstitutional in *Schechter Poultry Corporation v. United States*. The Brooklyn, New York, company had challenged the NRA's legality after the agency caused the poultrymen to be indicted for having violated NRA regulations on employee wages and hours. The high court ruled that Congress had no constitutional right to delegate to the NRA the authority to make laws, a direct reference to the codes of fair practice for various industries that the agency had drafted and on which the indictment had been based. The Court also used the Commerce clause of Article I of the Constitution to assert that the federal government had no power over Schechter anyway because the company was not engaged in interstate trade.

Although the majority decision was couched in legal terms, many historians believe the justices actually ruled against the Roosevelt administration because they were reluctant to strengthen the federal government and did not believe that Congress should enact legislation that made major changes in the way the nation was governed. The decision in what came to be called "the sick chicken case" not only voided the NRA but put in jeopardy the rule-making power that was at the heart of other New Deal agencies such as the Securities and Exchange Commission and the National Labor Relations Board. The high court made more decisions that hurt the New Deal and in 1937 was considering challenges to newer programs such as Social Security.

Although Franklin appears jubilant here, he was headed for political disaster with the announcement of the Judicial Reform Act, which gave the president new power in appointing federal and Supreme Court judges.

When his new term started in 1937, Roosevelt decided he had to do something to stop the high court from endangering his programs. It proved to be the biggest mistake of his presidency.

PACKING THE COURT

On February 5, 1937, Roosevelt announced the Judicial Reform Act. In essence, it gave the president the power to appoint a new federal judge for every judge who did not step down within six months after reaching the voluntary retirement age of seventy. Although he claimed the act would strengthen the judiciary by resulting in younger, more energetic judges who could handle more cases, everyone knew his real aim was to be able to "pack" the Supreme Court with justices favorable to his position. The retirement age affected six of the nine justices, including the four who were most conservative.

The measure was highly controversial, and not only because it would change the number of Supreme Court justices from nine, a figure many considered sacred. Many people were upset that Roosevelt had never mentioned the plan during his reelection campaign and that it would give him too much power because he would, in effect, control the judicial as well as the executive branch of federal government. In typical Roosevelt fashion, he took his case to the public in a fireside chat in early March:

> Our difficulty with the Court today arises not from the Court as an institution but from the human beings within it. We cannot yield our Constitutional destiny to the personal judgment of a few men who, being fearful of the future, would deny us the necessary means of dealing with the present.[73]

Roosevelt, however, was fighting one of the few political battles he would lose as president. Although many were sympathetic with Roosevelt's plight, the measure never got much congressional support and seemed doomed to be voted down. However, on March 29, the Supreme Court in a 5-4 decision upheld the minimum-wage law of the state of Washington, a stunning turnaround from its decision six months earlier to void a similar New York state law. Historians believe the timing of the decision indicates that justices were reacting defensively to Roosevelt's court-packing plan, which they feared would create a huge change in the Supreme Court. In the next few weeks the high court made several more decisions favorable to New Deal programs, including one on April 10 that declared the controversial new Labor Relations Act constitutional. Although it is impossible to know for sure, historian Cabell Phillips believes conservative justices caved in to pressure from Roosevelt to allow his programs to survive. Claims Phillips,

> Had the Nine Old Men [the Supreme Court justices] seen the light of day at last? We cannot be sure what prompted such an about-face in their philosophy, but henceforth they were to follow a much more liberal path. Their capitulation gave Roosevelt the substance of what he set out to achieve.[74]

The president soon gave up his court-packing scheme. But even though Roosevelt seemed to have gotten what he wanted, backing from the high court, it was a bitter defeat overall. His proposal would never have passed Congress, a severe blow to his pride, and he angered many people, supporters as well as enemies, by seeming to grab arrogantly for more power than he needed.

SECOND-TERM ACHIEVEMENTS

Roosevelt now returned to the business of being president, which was suddenly more difficult because a new economic slump had derailed recovery from the Great Depression. Many believe the economic downturn was caused by Roosevelt's decision to curb federal spending in 1937 to prevent inflation; his cuts in farm subsidies and other programs slowed the economy, and unemployment rose again to 10 million. Roosevelt proceeded to revive his New Deal programs to combat the new economic weakness.

In 1938 he called for $3 billion in new spending to create public works projects that would provide more jobs. He also reinvented his farm program by introducing a new Agricultural Adjustment Act to provide loans and raise farm prices based on soil conservation and other factors. In May 1938 he secured his last major

A political cartoon of the times lampoons Roosevelt's "packing the court" in an attempt to appoint judges with views similar to his own.

reform from Congress, the Fair Labor Standards Act. The labor bill was designed to help workers who were not protected by unions, and it basically replaced the now-scrapped NRA codes.

The new law established a 40-cent-per-hour minimum wage and a 40-hour maximum workweek, mandated time-and-a-half pay for overtime, and made child labor illegal in industries involved in interstate commerce. The law immediately provided important protection for 13 million workers, leading Roosevelt to declare it "the most far-reaching, far-sighted program for the benefit of workers ever adopted in this or any other country."[75] When its constitutionality was challenged, the Supreme Court upheld it unanimously.

PRESIDENTIAL RULES

In FDR's Splendid Deception, *author Hugh Gregory Gallagher, himself a victim of polio, describes how hard Roosevelt worked to try to make the public believe his disability was less severe than it was.*

"The White House imposed certain rules, which were always obeyed. For example, the president was never lifted in public. If it was necessary to lift him in or out of the car, this was done in the privacy of a garage or behind a temporary plywood screen constructed for the purpose. He was never seen in public seated in a wheelchair. Either he appeared standing, leaning on the arm of an aide, or he was seated in an ordinary chair. He required that the chair be solid enough to support his full weight as he pushed himself up to a standing position. Speaker podiums had to be solid and bolted to the floor. Once, in the 1932 campaign, this wasn't done, and the podium and the candidate crashed to the floor. Although reporters were present the incident was not mentioned in the press nor were pictures taken of his fall, although it was seen by photographers."

Gallagher also explains that the news media's hesitancy to portray the president's disability even extended to political cartoons, which appeared almost daily in newspapers across the country:

"FDR was their favorite subject for over twelve years, which is not surprising. But never once, so far as known, did they portray him in a wheelchair, on crutches, or as otherwise impaired. Instead, he was often shown as running, jumping, or even fighting in a boxing arena."

The influx of federal dollars again helped pump up the economy. And America was soon to be awash in a tidal wave of new money that would, once and for all, end the Great Depression. These funds, however, would be generated by the tragedy resulting from the start of a worldwide war.

WAR THREATENS

Five weeks before Roosevelt took the oath of office as president in 1932, Germany had gotten its own new leader. By 1939 this German chief of state, Adolf Hitler, had initiated a series of global incidents that would develop into a problem that was as difficult and dangerous for Roosevelt to deal with as the Great Depression had been—World War II.

Hitler had been elected for many of the same reasons as Roosevelt. Germany's economy had been shattered in the wake of its defeat in World War I, and millions of unemployed workers were searching for a leader who could offer them hope for the future. In America voters chose Roosevelt, a Progressive. In Germany, though, they turned to a fascist, Hitler, and his National Socialist (Nazi) Party. Within a few years, Hitler became an all-powerful dictator who was menacing the rest of Europe, forcibly annexing neighboring Austria in 1938 and seizing the Sudetenland, a section of Czechoslovakia that he claimed belonged to Germany. Hitler also began his relentless persecution of Jews, which began to shock and horrify the world.

Adolf Hitler, Germany's powerful and ruthless dictator, was only one of several world leaders whose policies threatened world peace.

The threat of war had also increased dramatically in other areas of the world since Roosevelt became president. Italian dictator Benito Mussolini had invaded Ethiopia and Albania; the militarists who ruled Japan had marched into China to begin their attempt to conquer all of Asia; and Francisco Franco was trying to overthrow Spain's democratic form of government.

At first Roosevelt was too concerned with helping his own country recover from the depression to do more than monitor the deteriorating situation in the rest of the world. But gradually Roosevelt realized he had to do something about the possibility of another war, which he hated. His visits to World War I battlefields in France and Belgium as assistant secretary of the navy had shocked him so much that he could say two decades later during his 1936 re-election campaign, "I have seen war. I have seen blood running from the wounded. I have seen men coughing through their gassed lungs. I hate war."[76]

Roosevelt, however, now found himself in the same awkward political position President Woodrow Wilson had been in when World War I began. Even though Roosevelt knew that the United States should enter the conflict on the side of democratic nations like England and France, he could not commit his country to a foreign war because most Americans wanted to stay out of conflicts involving other nations.

ISOLATIONISM

Ever since George Washington cautioned Americans to "steer clear of permanent alliances with any portion of the foreign world"[77] in his farewell address in 1796, the United States had favored a policy of isolation. Thus American presidents had tried to avoid becoming entangled in the affairs of other nations. After sitting on the sidelines for three years while World War I raged in Europe, America had finally helped England and France defeat Germany and the Austro-Hungarian Empire. But in the decades since then, America had

retreated again from the world stage, refusing to join the League of Nations—a short-lived organization Wilson had conceived to promote world peace—and trying to ignore the dire events that were occurring in Europe and in the Far East that would soon lead to another world war.

Partly because Roosevelt had focused his first term on dealing with the domestic crisis of the depression, he had refrained from vetoing a series of Neutrality Acts that isolationists pushed through Congress from 1935 to 1937. These laws prohibited America from trading with or giving credit to any nation at war.

But Roosevelt, who before America entered World War I had been one of the strongest advocates of U.S. involvement, now found it harder and harder to stand aside and do nothing while some more powerful nations began to prey on weaker countries. When Japan invaded China in 1937 he declared in Chicago on October 5 that

> The epidemic of world lawlessness [aggression by nations like Japan against other countries] is spreading. When an epidemic of physical disease starts to spread, the community approves and joins in a quarantine of the patients in order to protect the health of the community against the spread of disease. War is a contagion, whether it be declared or undeclared. There is no escape through mere isolation or neutrality. There must be positive endeavors to preserve peace.[78]

His call for action created a firestorm of negative reaction from Americans, with his severest critics labeling him a "warmonger." Roosevelt was so dismayed by the backlash that he proposed no measures to implement his own call for "positive endeavors." In fact, in December when the Japanese mistakenly sank a U.S. gunboat in China, the *Panay*, he meekly accepted their apology. Roosevelt later admitted he was saddened that his comments in Chicago had not convinced people action was needed: "It's a terrible thing to look over your shoulder when you are trying to lead and find no one there."[79]

In the summer of 1939 when it seemed inevitable that England and France would have to fight Germany, Roosevelt tried to get Congress to end the Neutrality Act's arms embargo so the United States could help the two nations. He lost because isolationist senators predicted there would be no war. But when Germany invaded Poland on September 1, the conflict did begin because Great Britain and France had mutual defense treaties with the beleaguered nation.

The conflict that would become known as World War II, which had already been raging for several years in the Far East, had now come to Europe. On September 3 Roosevelt reluctantly told the nation in one of his fireside chats that America, at least for now, would not directly join the conflict:

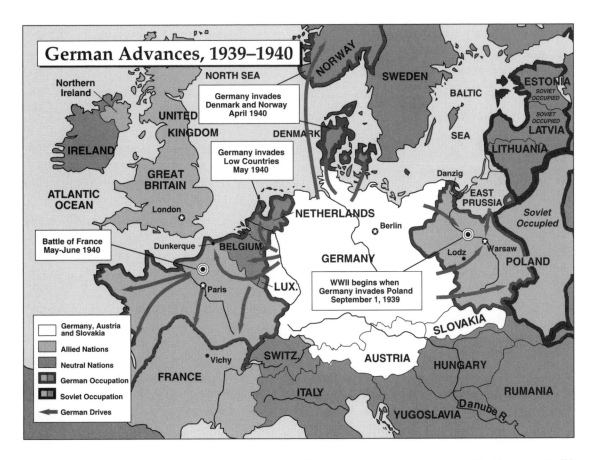

German Advances, 1939–1940

Northern Ireland

NORTH SEA

Germany invades Denmark and Norway April 1940

NORWAY

SWEDEN

BALTIC

ESTONIA
SOVIET OCCUPIED

SOVIET OCCUPIED

LATVIA

UNITED KINGDOM

DENMARK

SEA

LITHUANIA

IRELAND

Germany invades Low Countries May 1940

Danzig

ATLANTIC OCEAN

GREAT BRITAIN

London

NETHERLANDS

Berlin

EAST PRUSSIA

Soviet Occupied

Battle of France May–June 1940

Dunkerque

BELGIUM

GERMANY

Lodz

Warsaw

POLAND

Paris

LUX.

WWII begins when Germany invades Poland September 1, 1939

SLOVAKIA

Germany, Austria and Slovakia

Allied Nations

Neutral Nations

German Occupation

Soviet Occupation

German Drives

Vichy

SWITZ.

AUSTRIA

HUNGARY

FRANCE

ITALY

RUMANIA

Danube R.

YUGOSLAVIA

Roosevelt on the campaign trail. The actions of Hitler strongly influenced the president's decision to run for an unprecedented third term in office.

This nation will remain a neutral nation, but I cannot ask that every American remain neutral in thought as well. Even a neutral has a right to take account of facts. Even a neutral cannot be asked to close his mind or his conscience.[80]

Neither could Roosevelt, who already believed America needed to stop Germany or risk being overwhelmed by the military giant at a later date. Now all he had to do was convince the rest of the nation.

A THIRD TERM

George Washington had retired to his Virginia estate, Mount Vernon, after two terms as president, and no chief executive since had run for a third term. But in 1940 Roosevelt decided to break tradition once again by seeking reelection, and it was Hitler, more than anyone else, who prompted Roosevelt to try to become the first man ever elected president three

times. Roosevelt ran again because he was worried that whoever succeeded him, Democrat or Republican, might fail to act strongly enough to help America survive the coming calamity of World War II.

Roosevelt never formally campaigned for his party's nomination. But after delegates began chanting "WE WANT ROOSEVELT!" at the Democratic Convention in Chicago, his name was placed in nomination, and on the first ballot he received 946 votes, more than ten times the number for second-place James Farley, one of his political advisers. In accepting the nomination, Roosevelt explained why he was running for an unprecedented third term:

In the face of that public danger [war], all those who can be of service to the Republic have no choice but to offer themselves for service in those capacities for which they may be fitted. I had made plans for myself, plans for a private life, but my conscience will not let me turn my back on a call to service.[81]

6 FDR's Third Term: Battling Isolationists

No one did more than Franklin Roosevelt to prepare Americans for World War II or convince them it was time to scrap their isolationist attitudes and take a stand in the deadly conflicts being waged around the world. In his autobiographical *My Parents*, James Roosevelt recalled how his father once explained to him the slippery, precarious political tightrope he tread in trying to almost single-handedly make the nation realize its duty:

> Jimmy, I knew we were going to war. I was sure there was no way out of it. I had to delay [U.S. entry] until there was no way out of it. I knew we were woefully unprepared for war and I had to begin a buildup for what was coming. But I couldn't come out and say a war was coming, because the people would have panicked and turned from me. I had to educate the people to the inevitable, gradually, step by step, laying the groundwork for programs which would allow us to prepare for the war that was drawing us into it.[82]

The fact that 1940 was an election year made his task all the harder.

THE 1940 CAMPAIGN

The Republicans nominated Wendell Willkie, a corporate lawyer who had never held office. Even though Willkie supported most of Roosevelt's foreign and domestic policies, the campaign became bitter and divisive. Roosevelt was accused of trying to become a dictator for seeking a third term, leading to billboards with bizarre messages such as "SAVE YOUR CHURCH. DICTATORS HATE RELIGION."[83]

What part America would play in the war became the campaign's overriding issue. The isolationist America First Committee was formed to challenge Roosevelt's foreign policy. The Republican National Committee attacked Roosevelt with such insensitivity that radio ads like this one actually created sympathy for Roosevelt: "When your boy is dying on some battlefield in Europe and he's crying out, 'Mother! Mother!'—don't blame Franklin D. Roosevelt because he sent your boy to war—blame YOURSELF because YOU sent Franklin D. Roosevelt back to the White House!"[84]

Roosevelt campaigned little at first, claiming he had to remain in Washington

Wendell Willkie, the politically inexperienced Republican presidential candidate in 1940, speaks at a campaign rally.

so he could respond to emergencies overseas, but he finally began making speeches in key cities. One of his most important was in Boston on October 30, when he confronted the worst fear Americans had about war:

> And while I am talking to you mothers and fathers, I give you one more assurance. I have said this before, but I shall say it again and again and again: Your boys are not going to be sent into any foreign wars. They are going into training to form a force so strong that by its very existence, it will keep the threat of war away from our shores.[85]

The president had made that promise before, but always with the provisional phrase "except in case of attack." Willkie was furious that Roosevelt had deleted that disclaimer, calling him "that hypocritical son of a bitch!" and predicting, "This is going to beat me."[86] Willkie was right. Almost surely, Roosevelt was not being honest with voters—by then, he must have believed the country would have to enter the war—and on November 5 Roosevelt was elected to a historic third term.

INFLUENCING AMERICA

The role Franklin D. Roosevelt played in trying to convince Americans they needed to take part in World War II was not only difficult but delicate. He had to act strongly so that he would not disappoint people who were already on his side, but not act so dramatically that he would anger isolationists enough to create a backlash against what he was trying to accomplish. In The Glory and the Dream: A Narrative History of America 1932–1972, *historian William Manchester writes that Roosevelt sometimes moved too slowly for people who agreed with him.*

"[Connecticut congresswoman] Clare Boothe Luce, who thought the President should be tougher with Hitler, accused him of waging a 'soft war.' Every leader has his symbolic gesture, she said: Churchill's fingered V, Hitler's stiff arm, Mussolini's strut. When she was asked about Roosevelt, she moistened her finger and held it up to test the wind. It was clever, it was true, and it was absolutely necessary. The president had to know how Americans felt. Divided countries do not win great wars. He could be a step ahead of the people, perhaps even two steps. But if he ever lost them he would fail them and his oath of office. 'To serve the public faithfully, and at the same time please it entirely,' Benjamin Franklin wrote, 'is impossible.'"

Manchester explains that, because Roosevelt did take public opinion into account when he acted, the president's policy sometimes shifted back and forth from being very strong to being weak in reaction to what was happening overseas. But overall, Manchester said, Roosevelt kept faithfully to his mission to make America stronger and do its duty to the rest of the world.

"The president was under intense pressure from extremists at both ends of the spectrum; it came from Congressional leaders, aides, cabinet members; even from his wife. In retrospect, his policy seems clearer [today] than it did then. He was giving Britain everything he could lay his hands on. He was mobilizing American industry and arming the country to the teeth."

Roosevelt received 4 million more votes than Willkie and had a landslide 449-82 edge in the Electoral College. Another set of numbers shows how effective Roosevelt was in changing U.S. sentiment about the war. Three times during 1940, the Gallup poll asked Americans if they wanted to stay out of the conflict in Europe or do everything possible to help Great Britain, even at the risk of going to war. Although in May 64 percent of Americans wanted to "stay out" while 36 percent wanted to "help England," by November the numbers had evened at 50-50, and by December only 40 percent maintained the isolationist position.

PREPARING FOR WAR

Roosevelt, however, was only one factor in changing public opinion. Americans were horrified as well as awed by the success German armies had in the spring of 1940 as they swept across Europe in the blitzkrieg (lightning war), conquering nation after nation and leaving Great Britain the last remaining European democracy. In August German planes began raining bombs on English cities in the Battle of Britain, and Adolf Hitler began planning an invasion across the English Channel.

On June 22 the fall of France, an old and valued ally, had led Americans to start fearing for their own safety. This enabled Roosevelt to win congressional approval by September for the first peacetime draft in U.S. history (America at the time ranked nineteenth in world military power with only a half-million soldiers,

one-twelfth the number Hitler had). He was also given $17 billion to rearm the nation so it could defend itself.

Stymied by the Neutrality Act, Roosevelt used his power as president to trade fifty destroyers to Great Britain in exchange for leases on naval and air bases in the British West Indies, Argentia Bay (Newfoundland), and Bermuda. The British desperately needed the ships to attack German submarines, which were sinking ships carrying armaments and other supplies from America. Although the destroyers were a minor factor in the overall situation, many historians believe America's willingness to act at that key moment helped make Hitler decide against invading England.

Roosevelt viewed his reelection as a mandate to help Great Britain. In a news conference on December 17, he unveiled a plan to lend or lease weapons and supplies to any nation whose defense was vital to that of America's security. Lend-lease was needed because Great Britain was broke and could no longer buy the weapons, ammunition, warships, and airplanes it needed to continue fighting. In a news conference, Roosevelt explained the issue in simple terms people could understand:

Suppose my neighbor's house catches fire, and I have a length of garden hose. If he can take my garden hose and connect it up with his hydrant, I may help him put out the fire. Now what do I do? I don't say to him before that operation, "Neighbor, my garden hose cost me fifteen dollars; you have to pay me fifteen dollars for it." What

Queen Elizabeth surveys bomb damage in England. Roosevelt felt that his reelection was a mandate to help Great Britain, the only remaining democracy in Europe.

is the transaction that goes on? I don't want fifteen dollars—I want my garden hose back after the fire is over.[87]

It was an intriguing analogy but one with a fatal flaw; the "hose"—actually planes and other weapons the United States would supply—would probably be destroyed and never returned. In January 1941, when Roosevelt proposed the Lend-Lease Act, it was bitterly opposed by isolationists like Sena-

tor Burton K. Wheeler. The Montana lawmaker claimed U.S. involvement would "plow under every fourth American boy" by having them die in the fighting, to which Roosevelt angrily responded to reporters: "That is really the rottenest thing that has ever been said in public life in my generation. Quote me on that."[88]

But Roosevelt's homespun reasoning had put public opinion on his side, and Congress approved the Lend-Lease Act

Roosevelt's Four Freedoms

When Franklin D. Roosevelt delivered his annual message to Congress on January 6, 1941, Great Britain's defeat by Germany seemed very possible because of the massive air attacks known as "the Blitz." Roosevelt used his speech to point out that, unless the United States acted to save countries like England, the freedom that Americans valued so highly would be imperiled around the world. The speech appears on the Franklin and Eleanor Roosevelt Institute website.

"Every realist knows that the democratic way of life is at this moment being directly assailed in every part of the world—assailed either by arms, or by secret spreading of poisonous propaganda by those who seek to destroy unity and promote discord in nations that are still at peace. Therefore, as your President, performing my constitutional duty to 'give to the Congress information of the state of the Union,' I find it, unhappily, necessary to report that the future and the safety of our country and of our democracy are overwhelmingly involved in events far beyond our borders."

Roosevelt argued that the United States needed to act to help ensure what he called the "Four Freedoms" for both America and the rest of the world.

"In the future days, which we seek to make secure, we look forward to a world founded upon four essential human freedoms. The first is freedom of speech and expression—everywhere in the world. The second is freedom of every person to worship God in his own way—everywhere in the world. The third is freedom from want—which, translated into world terms, means economic understandings which will secure to every nation a healthy peacetime life for its inhabitants—everywhere in the world. The fourth is freedom from fear—which, translated into world terms, means a world-wide reduction of armaments to such a point and in such a thorough fashion that no nation will be in a position to commit an act of physical aggression against any neighbor—anywhere in the world. That is no vision of a distant millennium. It is a definite basis for a kind of world attainable in our own time and generation. That kind of world is the very antithesis of the so-called new order of tyranny which the dictators seek to create with the crash of a bomb."

in March. Congress initially appropriated $7 billion, and the United States eventually dispatched $50 billion in defense goods to its allies to help win the war.

ARSENAL OF DEMOCRACY

America had become, in Roosevelt's words, "the great arsenal of democracy."[89] This meant the United States could manufacture the guns, tanks, planes, and ships Great Britain needed to continue fighting. This was not only good news for England but for America as well, because massive war spending by both the United States and England would finally end the Great Depression. Although 9 million Americans were unemployed at the end of 1940, the war was creating hundreds of new jobs daily and by late 1942 there were fewer than 1 million jobless workers, giving the country its lowest unemployment rate in over a decade.

Despite U.S. help to England, the situation was still bleak. Hitler's armies in 1941 overran Greece and Yugoslavia and invaded North Africa and Egypt while Japan continued its conquest of China. On June 22 Hitler also decided to invade the Soviet Union, which had initially helped Germany subdue Poland. Attacking the Soviet Union was one of the most critical decisions of the war, and it would backfire on Hitler. Unable to subdue the Soviets with its initial offensive, Germany would now have to wage war on two fronts, east and west.

Russia had been an enemy of the United States since the Communist takeover in 1917, but an old adage reasons that "the enemy of my enemy is my friend." Even though it was politically unpopular, Roosevelt decided on June 24 to extend lend-lease aid to the Soviets, claiming, "I deem it to be of paramount importance for the safety and security of America that reasonable help be provided for Russia."[90]

In addition to helping other nations, the United States began gearing up for war itself by drafting hundreds of thousands of soldiers and sailors and molding them into a force that could defend America. In August the president met in Newfoundland with British prime minister Winston Churchill and signed a joint agreement proclaiming an Atlantic Charter to ensure self-determination for all nations. Roosevelt also began to take a more offensive stance in the war, ordering naval vessels protecting U.S. merchant ships going to England to "shoot on sight" at German submarines, which were sinking the ships carrying supplies that England desperately needed to keep fighting.

The Germans had done the same thing in World War I, and it had been their continued submarine attacks on U.S. ships that finally led the United States to declare war on Germany. As a navy assistant secretary, Roosevelt had continually pushed President Woodrow Wilson to enter the war, only to have Wilson explain why he kept waiting:

> I want history to show not only that we have tried every diplomatic means to keep out of the war; to show that war has been forced upon us deliberately

ROOSEVELT AND CHURCHILL

In August 1941 Franklin D. Roosevelt and Winston Churchill met for the first time in Argentia Bay, Newfoundland. The two leaders had already come to respect each other in the communications they had exchanged for several years by letter, cable, and transatlantic telephone. On August 14 they issued a joint declaration of their war aims, which came to be known as the Atlantic Charter. They pledged to help defeat aggressor nations like Germany and to work for world peace when the fighting was over. But in F.D.R.: An Intimate History, *author Nathan Miller claims that something equally as important happened in the three days of meetings held on warships of the two nations. Roosevelt and Churchill became friends, forming perhaps the most important single relationship of the war. Miller explains the two men's relationship.*

"Roosevelt and Churchill were proud, even vain men, conscious of their responsibilities and places in history, but they took an immediate liking to each other. Sometimes during their meetings over the next four years, the President's garrulity [talkativeness] and determination to liquidate the British Empire [Roosevelt opposed colonialism, in which countries like Great Britain dominated other nations economically and politically] irritated Churchill, while the Prime Minister's passion for long speeches and late hours ruffled Roosevelt. Yet they were drawn to each other not only by the necessities of policy but by mutual admiration. 'It is fun to be in the same decade with you,' Roosevelt once cabled Churchill. And Churchill likened Roosevelt's sparkling buoyancy to uncorking a bottle of champagne. It was not a relationship of equals, however, and Roosevelt held most of the cards. Churchill was forced to woo the President, first to enter the war on Britain's side and then to support British policy. Although he was the older man, he chose to address Roosevelt as 'Mr. President'; Roosevelt called him 'Winston.'"

English prime minister Winston Churchill (right) and Roosevelt share a relaxed moment on the British battleship Prince of Wales.

by Germany; but also that we have come into the court of history with clean hands.[91]

Roosevelt now found himself in the same plight. He did not want to go to war until America was pushed into it irrevocably. Otherwise, the president feared, Americans would not unite to win the war, and without unity he was worried the nation might lose. Roosevelt refrained from declaring war even in October 1941 when a German submarine sank the U.S. destroyer *Reuben James*, killing 115 Americans.

JAPANESE CONQUEST

Until 1941 the fighting in Europe had drawn most of America's attention, but Roosevelt now became increasingly concerned about Japanese aggression. After conquering most of China, Japan in July 1941 invaded French Indochina (present-day Vietnam) and announced its intention to take control of the Philippines and other nations. Roosevelt had warned Japan not to attack Indochina, and in response he froze Japanese assets in U.S. banks and cut off shipments of scrap iron, steel, and petroleum. The island nation needed those supplies to wage war—80 percent of its oil, for example, came from America—and the sales embargo weakened Japan.

In the next few months, Japanese leaders tried to persuade Roosevelt to accept their plans for a "new order," a phrase that meant Japan would control all of Asia and most of the Pacific. When the president refused, War Minister Hideki Tojo

said the only course of action Japan had left was to "break through the military and economic"[92] barrier America had erected. Japan would do this by destroying one of the main tenets of isolationists—that they could ignore world affairs because the Atlantic and Pacific Oceans protected them from harm.

PEARL HARBOR

The morning of December 7 was typically sunny and warm on Oahu, one of the islands that in 1941 was a U.S. territory but today is part of the fiftieth state of Hawaii. Shortly before 8:00 A.M., this tranquil paradise was transformed into a living hell when hundreds of airplanes launched from Japanese aircraft carriers more than two hundred miles away began bombing Pearl Harbor, the U.S. Pacific Fleet's main naval base.

In only two hours, this sneak attack—one of the most daring but shameful in military history—killed 2,403 American sailors, soldiers, marines, and civilians; wounded 1,178 more people; destroyed 188 planes; and sank or damaged 18 ships. The aerial attack caught America by surprise. Although war between the two nations had appeared imminent, the Japanese had pretended to be interested in negotiating to resolve their disputes with the United States right up until the hour the bombs fell.

On December 8 while oily black smoke was still billowing skyward from the broken hulks of U.S. ships in Pearl Harbor, Roosevelt addressed a joint session of

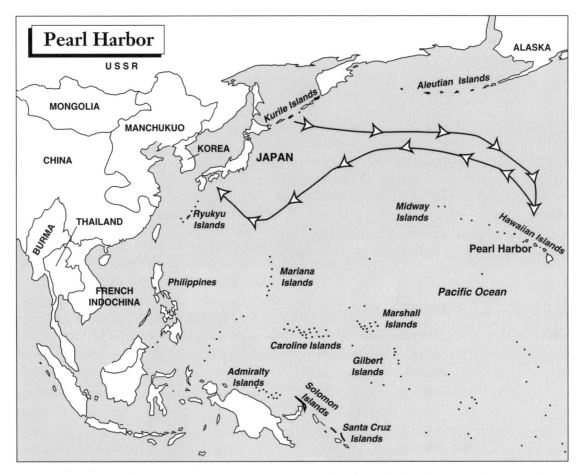

Pearl Harbor

Congress. He asked the Senate and House to declare war against Japan:

> Yesterday, December 7, 1941—a date which will live in infamy—the United States of America was suddenly and deliberately attacked by naval and air forces of the Empire of Japan.... No matter how long it may take us to overcome this premeditated invasion, the American people in their righteous might will win through to absolute victory. With confidence in our armed forces—with the unbounding determination of our people—we will gain the inevitable triumph—so help us God.[93]

The first draft of Roosevelt's speech referred to a date "which will live in history," but he changed "history" to "infamy" and created one of the most memorable of all presidential phrases. The Senate within an hour almost unanimously approved his request; the only "no" vote in the House was cast by Representative Jeannette Rankin, a Montana pacifist who had also opposed entering World War I. The declaration meant the United States would fight Germany and Italy as well as Japan, for on September 27, 1940, the three countries, which became known as the Axis Powers, had signed the Tripartite Pact, pledging to aid each other in case of attack by the United States.

JAPANESE MISCALCULATION

The Japanese had hoped that the crushing blow they delivered to U.S. military power would scare Americans so much that they would not fight. Instead, Pearl Harbor united the nation more strongly than it had ever been in support of one goal—victory in World War II. Even Wheeler, the arch isolationist who opposed Roosevelt's foreign policy, admitted, "The only thing to do now is to lick hell out of them."[94]

America's production capacity had been the key to winning World War I, when U.S. factories turned out guns, bullets, planes,

---

FDR AND PEARL HARBOR

Because U.S. intelligence had cracked the secret code the Japanese used to transmit diplomatic messages, President Roosevelt knew the day before the attack that Japan was going to break off peace talks with America and was likely to attack a U.S. possession somewhere in the Pacific. But no one knew where or when Japan would strike. In Franklin D. Roosevelt: A Rendezvous with Destiny, *FDR biographer Frank Freidel writes that, when Roosevelt reviewed the latest intercepted dispatches from Japan to its diplomatic office in Washington, D.C., on the night of December 6, 1941, he exclaimed, "This means war." But when Harry Hopkins, his top aide, said it was a shame "we could not strike the first blow and prevent any sort of surprise," the president remarked, "No, we can't do that. We are a democracy and a peaceful people." Critics of Roosevelt have suggested that he knew beforehand that Pearl Harbor was going to be Japan's target. But like most historians, Freidel believes such claims are ridiculous.*

"[Roosevelt's critics] began openly from 1945 on to circulate allegations, which in one form or other have persisted, that he was aware of the Japanese attack plans and concealed them from the commanders in Hawaii. They have charged that, unable to sway Congress and the public toward a declaration of war against Germany, he sacrificed the navy at Pearl Harbor to bring the United States into the hostilities through the back door. For Roosevelt thus to have acted would have been wholly out of character. He loved the navy. Had he not been president, he would have most wanted to be an admiral. Furthermore, as a father he faced the possibility of painful personal loss in a Pacific war. Of his four sons, two were officers in the navy, and one in the marines. As president and commander in chief, aware of the extreme difficulties and additional burdens war with Japan would create, he had sought, not without errors in judgment but with persistent earnestness, to avoid or at least postpone [war]."

---

and tanks, and American farmers had grown enough food to feed their own civilian and military populations as well as those from Allied countries. This American might, as well as the bravery of its soldiers, would also win World War II.

Japanese admiral Isoroku Yamamoto had been the military mastermind who conceived the innovative plan to attack Pearl Harbor. But even he had feared America's economic and production might, which he believed was so great that it would allow America to win any war against his country. In September 1940 Yamamoto told Japanese government officials, "If I am told to fight [against America]

regardless of the consequences, I shall run wild for the first six months or a year, but I have utterly no confidence for the second or third year. I hope you will endeavor to avoid a Japanese-American war."[95]

Yamamoto's prediction was devastatingly accurate. The attack on Pearl Harbor was the signal for a mighty offensive in which the Japanese in just a few months overcame U.S. forces guarding Wake Island, Guam, and the Philippines, forcing General Douglas MacArthur to flee for his life. The Japanese would conquer almost all of the South Pacific and threaten the safety of Australia before the United States could stop them.

Workers at an aircraft plant assemble warplanes. Japanese admiral Yamamoto feared the power of America's economic and production capabilities.

War Leader

Roosevelt would now play the most vital role of any Allied leader. His achievements are symbolized by two titles he held during the conflict. At home as "Dr. Win-the-War," Roosevelt coordinated the efforts of industry and labor to produce the weapons needed to battle the Axis Powers. He also kept citizens united and calm in the face of a foe even more powerful and terrifying than the Great Depression. Abroad, Roosevelt was hailed as "Commander-in-chief of the United Nations," a title that was not a reference to the organization that today tries to keep the peace worldwide (the United Nations was not founded until 1945) but to the nations that fought together and were known as the Allies.

Biographer Nathan Miller claims that "Roosevelt's greatness as a war leader lay in his ability to rally the people of the free world."[96] Pictures of Roosevelt printed in newspapers in many countries, his ever-present cigarette holder clenched in his teeth at a jaunty angle, were as reassuring a symbol of ultimate victory as Churchill's famous two-fingered "V" for victory salute. It was also Roosevelt who led the wartime alliance of powerful leaders like England's Churchill and the Soviet Union's Joseph Stalin, who disliked each other, and resolved differences that arose between them as they conducted a war spread over three continents and two oceans. Collectively with Roosevelt, these two leaders became known as the "Big Three."

The demands of leading a nation into war were heavier than any Roosevelt had ever borne. Although Roosevelt exulted in meeting the severe challenge, his life during the war was a sad one, and his son James wrote, "Father often spoke of how lonely he was during the war years."[97]

The president's beloved mother, Sara, had died September 6, 1940, and his four sons had all enlisted in the armed forces. Eleanor was away most of the time making speeches, inspecting military facilities, and being active in many social causes. Roosevelt was also now denied the companionship of Marguerite "Missy" LeHand, the secretary who had served him faithfully since 1920 and of whom White House aide Raymond Moley once said, "There's no doubt that Missy was as close to being a wife as he ever had—or could have."[98]

Companions

Although Roosevelt had broken off his affair with Lucy Mercer, he met LeHand when she worked on his 1920 vice presidential campaign. Roosevelt hired her as his secretary, and she remained at his side until June 1940, when she suffered a stroke. She would die in 1944. LeHand not only did secretarial duties for Roosevelt but helped run his household and served as a hostess when Eleanor was away, circumstances unusual enough to merit a comment in a 1938 *Saturday Evening Post* magazine article. LeHand was the light-hearted companion Eleanor could never be, helping Roosevelt manage his stamp collection, playing poker with him, and consoling him when he felt down. It was to LeHand that he had confided his deepest

Roosevelt's longtime secretary Marguerite LeHand was an excellent employee and also a helpmate in many other capacities.

fears during the long years he spent trying to recover from polio.

Roosevelt was often alone, but his married daughter, Anna, sometimes stayed at the White House and served as his hostess for important social occasions. Two unmarried cousins, Laura Delano and Margaret Suckley, also became frequent visitors to the White House. In the little free time Roosevelt had, he swam in a pool built for him in the White House. He also returned often to Warm Springs, residing in a small home that became known as the "Little White House," and enjoyed getaways to his childhood home in Hyde Park and to "Shangri-La," a rural retreat sixty-five miles from Washington in the Catocin Hills of Maryland where he could relax and fish.

CONFIDENCE

The war years were the most difficult of Roosevelt's presidency. The decisions he made affected not only his nation and millions of Americans who were fighting but the entire world. It was a tremendous burden, but one that was bearable because of his tremendous self-confidence, first instilled in him by his parents. Roosevelt once told a friend,

> I'll tell you, at night when I lay my head on my pillow, and it is often pretty late, and I think of the things that have come before me during the day and the decisions that I have made, I say to myself—well, I have done the best I could and turn over and go to sleep.[99]

Chapter

7 Winning a War, Striving for Peace

Franklin D. Roosevelt always remembered what a forlorn, tragic figure Woodrow Wilson had been when he visited the ailing president during the 1920 election campaign to promise his support for the League of Nations. "As we came in sight of the [White House] portico," Roosevelt said years later, "we saw the president in a wheel chair, his left shoulder covered with a shawl which concealed his left arm which was paralyzed."[100] Wilson had suffered a stroke in 1918 during his whirlwind national campaign to persuade America to join the league, a battle he ultimately lost to Senate isolationists.

Two decades later as World War II dragged on through Roosevelt's third term, this scene was being eerily reenacted in the White House. Only this time Roosevelt was the ailing president, a shrunken figure in a wheelchair often clad in a naval cape much like Wilson's shawl, who now received his own visits from well wishers and supporters who feared for his health.

Advancing age—in 1944 Roosevelt was sixty-two but looked much older and frailer—and the heavy burden of war were beginning to accomplish what polio could not. They were destroying Roosevelt physically. But before Roosevelt died, he would win a fourth term as president, lead the Allies to the brink of victory, and lay the groundwork for the global alliance to prevent future wars that Wilson had only dreamed about.

MOBILIZING AMERICA

The first months of 1942 were the scariest of the war for Americans. The Japanese advanced mightily through the Pacific, sweeping aside British and U.S. forces to conquer the Philippines, Malaya, Singapore, Burma, and New Guinea and threaten Australia. In Europe, Great Britain was being pounded unmercifully by waves of German planes, and the Soviet Union was locked in a bloody, stalemated battle with German troops on Russian soil.

Roosevelt knew that America's production capacity, greater than that of all the Axis Powers combined, held the key to victory as it had in World War I. And Congress in late December 1941 had passed the War Powers Act, giving him the tools to mobilize this economic might by managing U.S. industrial output from raw material to finished product. His administration could now allocate precious materials like steel,

Women work in an airplane manufacturing plant. Roosevelt knew that the production capabilities of America's workers and industries were key to winning the war.

rubber, and aluminum to factories and shipyards, establish priorities for what they should produce, and take them over if they did not perform adequately. To accomplish this and to manage other aspects of the nation's wartime economy, the president created agencies such as the War Production Board, Office of Price Administration, and Office of Price Stabilization.

Knowing he needed the cooperation of workers as well as industry, Roosevelt met with labor leaders and persuaded them to promise not to strike. In return the president said he would make sure workers were treated fairly. As a result there was only limited labor unrest that interrupted the flow of war matériel to American troops and Allied forces.

In early 1942 Roosevelt established initial U.S. quotas for planes, tanks, and other hardware, explaining that he expected American factories and workers to produce "a crushing superiority of equipment"[101] to defeat the Axis Powers. U.S. factories, shipyards, and workers did not let him down, manufacturing almost 300,000 military planes, 86,000 tanks, 71,000 naval ships, 3 million machine guns, and 55 million tons of merchant shipping. U.S. farmers also grew more food than ever, enabling America to help feed its allies as well as its own citizens and soldiers.

The president's prodding efforts to prepare the nation for war, especially the creation of the draft, had already begun to increase U.S. military strength before

Pearl Harbor. Once the bombs fell, the armed forces grew explosively, with thousands of patriotic young Americans flooding recruitment centers the day after the attack. In 1941 the U.S. military numbered only 1.6 million, a figure that in four years would balloon to more than 15.1 million men and women who would serve and die bravely in far corners of the world to win a conflict they now thought of as America's war.

DOMESTIC CHANGE

At home the tidal wave of war spending washed away the last vestiges of the Great Depression, providing jobs for everyone. Although *Time* magazine's boast that the nation was "getting suddenly rich—everywhere, all at once,"[102] was overblown, workers were making good wages for the first time in many years. By 1944 the average weekly earnings in manufacturing had

---

A PRESIDENTIAL PEP TALK

Americans had grown to love Roosevelt's fireside chats in the decade since he became president. On October 12, 1942, Roosevelt went on the air to tell Americans how proud he was of them for the good job they were doing to get ready for World War II. The speech appears on the website of the Mid-Hudson Regional Information Center.

"MY FELLOW AMERICANS: As you know, I have recently come back from a trip of inspection of camps and training stations and war factories. The main thing that I observed on this trip is not exactly news. It is the plain fact that the American people are united as never before in their determination to do a job and to do it well. This whole nation of one hundred and thirty million free men, women, and children is becoming one great fighting force. Some of us are soldiers or sailors, some of us are civilians. Some of us are fighting the war in airplanes five miles above the continent of Europe or the islands of the Pacific—and some of us are fighting it in mines deep down in the earth of Pennsylvania or Montana. A few of us are decorated with medals for heroic achievement, but all of us can have that deep and permanent inner satisfaction that comes from doing the best we know how—each of us playing an honorable part in the great struggle to save our democratic civilization. Whatever our individual circumstances or opportunities—we are all in it, and our spirit is good, and we Americans and our allies are going to win—and do not let anyone tell you anything different. That is the main thing that I saw on my trip around the country—unbeatable spirit."

---

nearly doubled in five years to $45.70 (a respectable wage in those days); farm income skyrocketed; and wages and profits in other professions increased dramatically.

The creation of thousands of jobs in new defense plants scattered around the country ignited the most massive wave of migration the nation had experienced since the nineteenth century, when pioneers traveled ever westward to settle new lands. By the end of 1945, more than 15 million people lived in a county different from the one they had resided in before Pearl Harbor. The population shift was fueled by young people moving from rural areas to cities in search of good-paying jobs in defense factories and by some 700,000 African Americans who left their homes in southern states, where segregation and discrimination were strongest, to seek jobs in defense plants in northern cities such as Chicago and in California. The latter migration, similar to that which took place in World War I but involving many more people, forever changed the nation's racial balance.

Roosevelt opened the way for this African American resettlement on June 25, 1942, when he signed Executive Order 8802, which prohibited job discrimination in defense plants and created the first Fair Employment Practices Commission. Roosevelt acted, however, only after African American labor leader A. Philip Randolph threatened a protest march in the nation's capital by 100,000 people. Randolph was angry that plants were refusing to hire African Americans for anything but menial jobs, a racist stance represented by this comment from the general manager of North American Aviation: "Negroes will be considered only as janitors."[103]

The president backed the rights of African Americans, often at the urging of Eleanor, who in this and other matters was always the more socially conscious of the two. He was sometimes slow in supporting them, however, because white southern Democrats who had helped elect him again and again generally opposed equal rights for African Americans. But Randolph's threat of a mass march demonstrated to Roosevelt that the time for strong executive action had arrived.

ALLIED LEADER

Although the conflict drastically altered the way Americans lived then and for decades to come, Roosevelt's main priority was leading the grand alliance of nations fighting the Axis on three continents and two oceans. He concentrated on mapping out overall military strategy, negotiating with Allied leaders, and planning for a lasting peace following the conflict.

Roosevelt assumed the reins of leadership in a meeting that began on December 22, 1941, when British prime minister Winston Churchill came to Washington, D.C., after America had entered the war. From the very start, Roosevelt aide Robert Sherwood wrote years later, the president served "notice on such men as Churchill and [British cabinet member Lord] Beaverbrook that [he] was the boss and Washington the headquarters of the joint war effort."[104] Roosevelt and Churchill worked out plans to have a coalition of

Roosevelt's Failure: Japanese Internment

Franklin D. Roosevelt is revered for fighting for freedom around the world. But one of his greatest failures as president came during World War II when he denied freedom to a group of people innocent of any wrongdoing—Japanese Americans. After Pearl Harbor, many Americans feared that anyone of Japanese descent was their enemy. The result was that almost 120,000 Japanese men, women, and children, most of them U.S. citizens who had been born in America and were living in California, were exiled for most of the war to remote prison camps in states like Idaho, Utah, and Wyoming. In Freedom from Fear, *historian David M. Kennedy describes the emotional hysteria that led to this injustice.*

"Facts were no protection against the building gale of fear and prejudice. [Newspaper columnist] Westbrook Pegler wrote: 'The Japanese in California should be under armed guard to the last man and woman right now and to hell with [constitutional rights] until the danger is over.' Unapologetically racist voices joined the chorus. A leader of California's Grower-Shipper Vegetable Association declared, 'We might as well be honest. It's a question of whether the white man lives on the Pacific Coast or the brown man.' [West Coast military commander General John L.] DeWitt announced, 'A Jap's a Jap. It makes no difference whether he is an American citizen or not. I don't want any of them.'"

Japanese immigrants had been victims of racism in America since the nineteenth century. Kennedy explains that although Roosevelt was usually a defender of civil rights, he abandoned those principles now because he believed it was necessary.

"On February 19 [1942] Roosevelt signed Executive Order 9066. It directed the War Department to 'prescribe military areas from which any and all persons may be excluded.' No explicit reference to the Japanese was necessary. When [Attorney General Francis] Biddle objected that the order was 'ill-advised, unnecessary, and unnecessarily cruel,' Roosevelt silenced him with the rejoinder: 'This must be a military decision.'"

more than twenty nations both large (China) and small (Honduras) join forces to fight the Axis.

Although they were generally known as the Allies, Roosevelt coined a name for them at the end of the conference on January 1, 1942. The countries fighting Germany and Japan, Roosevelt announced, would be called the "United Nations," a phrase that in a few years would gain new meaning as the name for the new worldwide organization that would strive to prevent future wars. As "Commander-in-chief of the United Nations," Roosevelt had the difficult task of reconciling differences between Allied leaders. For example, while Soviet premier Joseph Stalin in 1942 wanted an immediate invasion of Europe because it would force Germany to pull troops away from the battle raging in his own country, Churchill was more concerned about saving British possessions halfway around the world such as India. Roosevelt, who opposed British colonialism, said he would help defend India from Japan but only if Great Britain would agree to allow it to become free after the war. Churchill eventually agreed, paving the way for that country's independence.

Roosevelt decided that the top priority should be defeating Germany. But his wish for an immediate attack against Germany across the English Channel—a desire shared by Stalin—would be put off for two years, partly because Churchill feared the Allies were not yet strong enough to invade France. Instead, the first great Allied landing came in November 1942 when U.S. and British forces challenged Germany by invading North Africa. For the first time, Hitler's armies were defeated, and the victory paved the way for more direct Allied attacks on Europe in 1943 and 1944.

The president did not forget Japan. After Pearl Harbor, Roosevelt demanded the U.S. military strike back quickly against Japan to help boost the morale of frightened Americans. On April 18, 1942, sixteen bombers took off from aircraft carriers near Japan and attacked Tokyo. Although the planes ran short of fuel and crashed in China, only nine of the eighty men under the command of Lieutenant Colonel James Doolittle died. The attack allowed Roosevelt to brag to Churchill and the American people, "We have had a good crack at Japan by air."[105] And in May and June 1942, U.S. naval forces defeated the Japanese in two crucial battles, the Coral Sea and Midway, to finally blunt that country's smashing offensive drive through the Pacific. U.S. aircraft carriers, still afloat because they were at sea on maneuvers when Pearl Harbor was attacked, played a key role in the victories.

Traveling President

To lead the Allies properly, Roosevelt in 1943 convened four major conferences on three continents so he could meet with Churchill, Stalin, China's Chiang Kai-shek, and other officials. Thus Roosevelt became the first president to leave the country in time of war and the first since Abraham Lincoln to visit an active war zone.

Roosevelt left on the first of these trips on January 9, boarding the presidential train at a secret siding near the Bureau of Engraving and Printing for a trip by rail to Miami, where he boarded a plane to begin a six-thousand-mile journey to Casablanca in Morocco. The president's trips abroad had to be conducted in great secrecy; if the enemy knew where he was going, they would have tried to kill him. To the president's delight, his sons Elliott and Franklin Jr., who were in the service, were on hand to greet him when he landed in Casablanca.

During the conference from January 12 to 24, the English persuaded Roosevelt to delay the invasion of France until 1944 and instead attack Sicily in July and Italy two months later. Both offensives were a success, forcing the ouster of dictator Benito Mussolini and Italy's surrender. To pacify Stalin over the delay in invading the European continent, Roosevelt increased shipments of war matériel to the Soviet Union. Roosevelt also announced at Casablanca that Germany and Japan would have to agree to unconditional surrender to end the war. World War I had ended after both sides negotiated an end to the fighting, but Roosevelt was determined to defeat them so thoroughly that they would never risk war again.

The Allies met again in May in Washington and made a major decision: to invade France the following spring from England. The British were still worried about whether such a daring attack across the English Channel could succeed and wanted to wait, but Roosevelt finally got his way. At another conference in August, this time in Quebec, Canada, Allied leaders finalized plans for the massive invasion, which was given the code name Operation Overlord. Included in the talks were military leaders from the ousted French government, including General Charles de Gaulle, who would later become president of France.

Roosevelt meets with Churchill. The British convinced the president to delay the invasion of France in order to first defeat Mussolini and Italy.

The conference in Tehran, Iran, from November 28 to December 1 was perhaps the most important of 1943 because it marked the first meeting between Roosevelt and Stalin. The journey from America was long and arduous for Roosevelt, who on November 21 stopped first in Cairo, Egypt, to rest and meet with Chiang Kai-shek. "We came in the back way," Roosevelt wrote in his diary of their complex flight plan, "so as to avoid German planes from the desert."[106]

After a meeting with the Chinese leader that accomplished little, Roosevelt flew to Tehran for the historic meeting with Stalin, whom he courted because he wanted Russian help against Japan when Germany was defeated. Roosevelt and Stalin even joined forces against Churchill, who again wanted to alter plans for Overlord. Although Roosevelt returned home still wary about Stalin, he was happy the Soviet leader had pledged to fight Japan. In a December 24 fireside chat, Roosevelt told Americans, "I believe he is truly representative of the heart and soul of Russia; and I believe that we are going to get along very well with him and the Russian people—very well indeed."[107]

THE 1944 ELECTION

Although most people took it for granted in 1944 that a commander in chief, even an

A meeting of three imposing world leaders: Stalin (left), Roosevelt, and Churchill pose for a photo in Tehran.

ailing one, would not step down in time of war, it was not a foregone conclusion that Roosevelt would run for a record fourth term. In an effort to stop him, Republicans started circulating rumors about Roosevelt's health and argued he was too ill to serve another term. Their claims were not entirely unfounded. The concerns of war, his travels, and his advancing age had all taken a heavy toll on Roosevelt.

In March 1944 the president, suffering from a wracking cough, had a physical examination that showed his heart was enlarged; his blood pressure was higher than normal, as it had been for years; and he had acute bronchitis. Roosevelt, fatigued and obviously weaker than in the past, was ordered to get more rest, limit his pack-a-day cigarette habit to six each day, and reduce fat and salt in the foods he ate. The diet resulted in a loss of twenty pounds, but the weight reduction made him look weaker and older. Even his own staff worried about him. His hands often shook as he smoked, he was becoming forgetful, and he was no longer able to stand, even with his braces.

Even though Roosevelt admitted "All that is within me cries to go back to my home on the Hudson River," he said that if he was nominated, "as a good soldier I will accept and serve."[108] He easily won the Democratic nomination and in his acceptance speech, Roosevelt explained the choice voters had to make between him and New York governor Thomas E. Dewey, the Republican candidate:

The people of the United States will decide this fall whether they wish to turn over this 1944 job—this worldwide job—to inexperienced and immature hands or whether they wish to leave it to those who saw the danger from abroad.[109]

In a newspaper picture taken while Roosevelt was delivering the speech, the president appears sick and old. But on election day, November 7, Americans, deciding that his experience was needed in time of war, returned him to office; he defeated Dewey by 3.6 million votes and enjoyed another Electoral College landslide, 432–99.

Roosevelt delivered his fourth inaugural address from the White House portico on January 20, 1945. In a brief and somber speech, he stressed the importance in the future for America to continue working with other nations:

We have learned that we cannot live alone, at peace; that our own well-being is dependent upon the well-being of other nations far away. We have learned that we must live as men and not as ostriches, nor as dogs in the mangers. We have learned to be citizens of the world, members of the human community.[110]

YALTA

During the war, Roosevelt's main concern beyond winning had been to create an organization that would ensure world peace. In October 1943 Roosevelt had persuaded foreign ministers of the Allied nations to sign an agreement to create the United Nations, and in 1944 they met in Washington, D.C., to work out the details of the new

Churchill (left), Roosevelt, and Stalin meet at Yalta. Victories against Japan and Germany seem assured as the world leaders discuss the post-war world.

organization, which was to hold its first sessions in San Francisco in April 1945. It was with the same desire to create a new world order of lasting peace that Roosevelt slipped out of Washington two days after his inauguration for one of the most momentous meetings of the war, a conference with Churchill and Stalin at Yalta, an ancient Russian resort on the Black Sea.

The meeting was not held to wage war but to plan the postwar world. Since the successful "D day" landing of Operation Overlord on June 6, 1944, Allied forces had

been pushing the German army back through occupied territory and were hurrying to meet up with the advancing Soviets in Berlin. In the Pacific, Allied forces had captured island after island and were bombing Japan daily. Victory in both theaters of war seemed assured, especially because Roosevelt was counting on the successful development of a deadly new weapon he had commissioned scientists to make—the atomic bomb. Roosevelt went to Yalta hoping to commit the Allies to supporting policies that would create a peaceful

FALA

One of the highlights of the 1944 presidential campaign was a September 23 appearance by Franklin D. Roosevelt before a labor union. Looking and sounding stronger than in recent months, Roosevelt delivered a blistering attack against his opponents. The most remembered part of his speech was his reference to Fala, his pet Scottish terrier. This excerpt appears in Franklin D. Roosevelt: Portrait of a President *by Joseph Gies.*

"These Republican leaders have not been content with attacks on me, or my wife, or on my sons. No, not content with that, they now include my little dog Fala. Well, of course, I don't resent attacks, and my family doesn't resent attacks, but Fala does resent them. You know, Fala is Scotch, and being a Scottie, as soon as he learned that the Republican fiction writers in Congress had concocted a story that I had left him behind on the Aleutian Islands and had sent a destroyer back to find him—at a cost to the taxpayers of two or three, or eight or twenty million dollars—his Scotch soul was furious. I am accustomed to hearing malicious falsehoods about myself, such as that old worm-eaten chestnut that I have represented myself as indispensable. But I think I have a right to resent, to object to libelous statements about my dog."

Roosevelt himself had written the remarks, which he delivered comically to the delight of his audience. His deft use of humor was in sharp contrast to his bland Republican foe, Thomas Dewey. The speech, heard by millions on radio, served to make people realize that the president might be older and sicker, but he was still a force to be reckoned with.

Eleanor and Franklin relax with Fala, their famous Scottish terrier.

future and allow every nation to freely choose the type of government it wanted. But Roosevelt's hopes were seriously weakened because of one man—Stalin.

Pictures of Roosevelt at Yalta seated between Churchill and Stalin show a gaunt, tired old man, a cigarette clenched in one hand, his naval cape thrown over slumped shoulders. Many historians believe that Roosevelt, possibly because of his poor health, was outwitted in the talks by Stalin. During the meeting, which ran from February 4 to 12, the conferees worked out the details on how to treat Germany after the war and how to operate the United Nations. They also agreed in principle to a Declaration on Liberated Europe, which pledged them to allow nations ravaged by war to democratically choose the type of government they wanted.

But by driving back the Germans, the Russians had taken control of all of Eastern Europe, and Stalin hated to surrender any of the territory his army had won. Stalin wanted countries like Poland, Hungary, and Romania to become Communist satellite nations. At Yalta, Roosevelt and Stalin argued specifically over the fate of Poland, where Stalin had already installed a Communist government. In the end, Roosevelt backed down on Poland's future, accepting Stalin's promise to allow the citizens there to choose their own leaders freely even though he suspected that the Soviet dictator did not intend to honor his commitments. Roosevelt also approved agreements to return territory the Soviets had lost to Japan in the Russo-Japanese War of 1904–1905 if Russia would fight Japan once Germany was defeated.

Historians have criticized Roosevelt for allowing Stalin to lay the groundwork for his country's domination of Eastern Europe. However, Roosevelt wanted to make Russia a willing partner in the new United Nations and he was desperate to secure the Soviets' help in defeating Japan, something his military advisers assured him was vital. At the time, it was believed that subduing Japan would take many months of brutal fighting and that tens of thousands of U.S. soldiers would die. Although in just a few more months the atomic bomb would force Japan to quickly surrender without a prolonged invasion of its homeland, at Yalta the president was still not sure the new weapon would work.

Even Roosevelt realized he had not won the best possible terms in the negotiations. Commenting on Yalta, he told an aide, "I didn't say the result was good. I said it was the best I could get."[111]

FDR Reports

Roosevelt returned to Washington more tired than ever. But only twenty-eight hours after arriving home, on March 1, he appeared before Congress to tell them about his trip. He opened his speech in an unusual way:

> Mr. Vice President, Mr. Speaker, members of the Congress, I hope you will pardon me for the unusual posture of sitting down during the presentation of what I wish to say, but I know you will realize it makes it a lot easier for me in not having to carry about ten pounds of steel around the bottom of my legs.[112]

EINSTEIN'S LETTER TO FDR

On August 2, 1939, famed physicist Albert Einstein wrote a letter to Franklin D. Roosevelt that would help the United States defeat Japan. Soon after Adolf Hitler came to power in 1933, Einstein, who was Jewish, renounced his German citizenship and moved to the United States. Although Einstein hated war, his letter to Roosevelt (which appears on the website of the Public Broadcasting System) paved the way for the creation of the deadliest weapon in history, the atomic bomb.

"Sir: Some recent work by [physicists] E. [Enrico] Fermi and L. [Leo] Szilard, which has been communicated to me in manuscript, leads me to expect that the element uranium may be turned into a new and important source of energy in the immediate future. Certain aspects of the situation which has arisen seem to call for watchfulness and, if necessary, quick action on the part of the administration. I believe therefore that it is my duty to bring to your attention the following facts: In the course of the last four months it has been made probable—through the work of [scientists] in France as well as Fermi and Szilard in America—that it may become possible to set up a nuclear chain reaction in a large mass of uranium, by which vast amounts of power would be generated. Now it appears almost certain that this could be achieved in the immediate future. This new phenomenon would also lead to the construction of bombs, and it is conceivable—though much less certain—that extremely powerful bombs of a new type may thus be constructed. A single bomb of this type, carried by boat and exploded in a port, might very well destroy the whole port together with some of the surrounding territory. However, such bombs might very well prove to be too heavy for transportation by air."

Einstein also warned the president that the Germans were trying to develop this powerful new bomb. Roosevelt, who had the foresight to realize that whoever had such a weapon would win the war, began funding research into what became known as the Manhattan Project, the top-secret program that would result in the creation of the atomic bomb.

Albert Einstein

Roosevelt addresses Congress following the Yalta Conference. For the first time in public, the president mentions his disability.

Roosevelt's reference to his disability stunned those in attendance because in the past he had never referred to his physical problems. Congressmen also noticed how frail and sickly the president looked; he had trouble turning the pages of his speech and at times rambled on as he lost his train of thought. Despite being exhausted, the president continued working long hours in violation of doctors' orders. Finally giving in to requests to take it easy, he left Washington on March 28 for a much-needed rest at the "Little White House" in his beloved Warm Springs, Georgia.

On April 9 the president was joined by his old friend Lucy Mercer Rutherfurd and Elizabeth Shoumatoff, a friend Rutherfurd had commissioned to paint Roosevelt's portrait. Roosevelt's former lover had mar-

ried after he ended the affair, but they had kept in contact over the years and were friends. In the early afternoon of April 12, Roosevelt was trying to read documents his aides had brought while Shoumatoff was painting him.

Anxious to be done with the sitting that day, Roosevelt warned the painter, "We've got just fifteen minutes more."[113] Roosevelt then slipped a cigarette into his holder and lit it. Shoumatoff watched as the president began to squeeze his forehead several times and then said softly, "I have a terrific headache."[114] His left arm fell, his head dropped to the left, his chest slumped. It was 1:15 P.M. Roosevelt had just lapsed into unconsciousness after suffering a cerebral hemorrhage. Two hours later, he was declared dead.

FDR's Curious Legacy

When Franklin D. Roosevelt died, praise poured out of every city in America, every great capital around the world. At home, *Time* magazine editorialized that "Men will thank God on their knees a hundred years from now that [Roosevelt] was in the White House," and even one of his political foes, Republican senator Robert A. Taft, declared, "He dies a hero of the war, for he literally worked himself to death in the service of the American people."[115] Abroad, Great Britain's Winston Churchill wrote the widowed Eleanor that history would record "the glory of his name and the magnitude of his work," and even Japan, America's most bitter enemy, claimed to "grieve the death of President Roosevelt [at a time] when the whole world is in such a state of chaos."[116]

The night after Roosevelt died, thousands of people lined railroad tracks on the route back to Washington, bidding a tearful farewell to the dead president as the train carrying his body sped by in the dark. A small funeral service was held in the White House on April 14, and a second, even more private ceremony was held the following day at Hyde Park, where Roosevelt was buried in the rose garden where he had played as a boy.

Children look at a newspaper paying tribute to Roosevelt as they wait for his funeral procession to pass by.

A view of the devastation caused by the atomic bomb on Hiroshima.

Almost before the nation and world could comprehend what his death meant, Roosevelt had been laid to rest. Americans were stunned that the president who led them out of the Great Depression and to the brink of victory in World War II had so suddenly disappeared from their lives. But Adolf Berle, a trusted adviser, knew that Roosevelt's passing marked only the beginning of how he would be assessed by history:

> Great men have two lives, one which occurs while they work on this earth; the second which begins the day of their death and continues as long as their ideas and conceptions remain powerful.[117]

FOREIGN POLICY LEGACY

The dead president's immediate legacy was victory in World War II. Germany surrendered on May 7 and Japan on August 14 after the United States dropped atomic bombs on Hiroshima and Nagasaki. Roosevelt had been instrumental in developing the bomb, but it was his successor, President Harry Truman, who had to make the difficult decision to use this terrible new weapon. And on April 25, less than two weeks after Roosevelt's death, delegates from fifty nations had met in San Francisco to organize the United Nations, the organization he had helped create to prevent future wars. Roosevelt had hoped to leave his nation a legacy of peace that would last for generations.

His great wish never materialized because, before the fighting in World War II ended, conflicts arose with the Soviet Union that would escalate into a half-century of strife and contention known as the cold war. In the decades after his death, as America became mired in conflicts in Korea and Vietnam, critics claimed that Roosevelt was to blame because his decisions at Yalta had allowed the Soviets to become too strong by seizing Eastern Europe. But like most historians, Roosevelt biographer Nathan Miller believes there was nothing he could have done to stop the Soviets short of military action, which was simply unthinkable:

> As much as Roosevelt and Churchill may have wished for a free and independent Poland, the cardinal facts remain that the Red Army was in complete control of Eastern Europe. The only alternative for the United States and Britain [would have been] the use of military force to install a government more to their liking.[118]

Miller also notes that if Joseph Stalin had kept the promises he made at Yalta, Eastern Europe would not have become enslaved by the Communists. But before he died, even Roosevelt, who during the war had shown a naive faith in the dictator he kiddingly called "Uncle Joe," began to realize the Soviets could no longer be trusted. "We can't do business with Stalin," Roosevelt remarked to an aide on March 23, 1945. "He has broken every one of the promises he made at Yalta."[119]

Roosevelt's greatest foreign policy achievement was that he destroyed the isolationism that had gripped the nation for most of its first two centuries. The result was that the United States, now the most powerful nation on earth, would continue to pursue the world leadership role Roosevelt had created for it.

DOMESTIC LEGACY

Power is also at the heart of Roosevelt's domestic legacy—more power not only for the federal government but for the presidency itself. Presidential historian Michael P. Riccards claims that Roosevelt forever changed the nature of the office of chief executive:

> It is clear that in the twentieth century, the pre-eminent model [of the presidency] is one established by FDR himself—a change in scope of the office and the accessibility to the media, in the range of domestic concerns, and in the responsibilities of foreign policy. In a sense, all modern presidents are heirs of FDR.[120]

Before Roosevelt, Congress was more influential than the president in setting policy and making important decisions. Afterward, presidents had new power and latitude to act on their own in critical situations and to set the agenda for national action, often by appealing directly to Americans for their support on various issues, something that Roosevelt had done so often and so successfully through his fireside chats and other forums.

Roosevelt also greatly expanded the federal government's power to affect the daily lives of its citizens, something that was embodied in his New Deal legislation, which, even though failing to end the Great Depression, at least helped Americans to survive it. Many of the programs he began are still alive today, as is the emphasis he placed on the government's moral responsibility to help those in need. Roosevelt biographer Ted Morgan claims, "The country we are living in today is to a great extent of [Roosevelt's] making. He transformed America with programs like Social Security. The New Deal lives on in a hundred ways."[121]

THE DISABLED

Roosevelt also transformed the way Americans view people with physical disabilities. In 1921 when he contracted polio, even many of his friends and former associates believed his political career was over, that he was a "cripple" who was no longer capable of doing anything useful. On January 10, 2001, President Bill Clinton spoke at the Roosevelt Memorial in Washington, D.C., when a statue was unveiled that showed Roosevelt seated in a wheelchair.

The statue was added to the memorial because advocates for the disabled charged that the monument was trying to cover up his condition by failing to include any pictures or statues showing his disability. Clinton said the addition of a statue recognizing the physical problem Roosevelt overcame is an important symbol to the disabled as well as everyone:

> This is a monument to freedom, the power of every man and woman to transcend circumstance, to laugh in the face of fate, to make the most of what God has given them. The power of the statue is in its immediacy, and in its reminder to all who touch, all who see, all who walk or wheel around, that they, too, are free, but every person must claim freedom.[122]

AN EPITAPH

Historians have labored mightily to assess the long, brilliant presidency of Franklin Delano Roosevelt. But perhaps no one ever did it better than Roosevelt himself in a statement he made about another great president, Abraham Lincoln:

> I think the impression was that Lincoln was a pretty sad man, because he could not do all he wanted to do at one time, and I think you will find examples where Lincoln had to compromise to gain a little something. He had to compromise to make a few gains. Lincoln was one of those unfortunate people called a "politician," but he

President Clinton and the Roosevelt grandchildren at the Roosevelt Memorial ceremony. The controversial statue clearly shows Roosevelt's disability and serves as a symbol to the disabled and the entire nation.

was a politician who was practical enough to get a great many things done for this country. He was a sad man because he couldn't get it all at once. And nobody can.[123]

Like Lincoln, Roosevelt was a politician. Like Lincoln, he accomplished many great things, but not all that he wanted to. And like Lincoln, his failures often made him sad.

Notes

Introduction: Franklin D. Roosevelt: Breaking Tradition

1. Quoted in Nathan Miller, *F.D.R.: An Intimate History.* Garden City, NY: Doubleday, 1983, p. 278.

2. Quoted in Doris Kearns Goodwin, "Franklin D. Roosevelt." www.pbs.org/newshour/character/essays/roosevelt.html.

3. Quoted in David M. Kennedy, *Freedom from Fear: The American People in Depression and War, 1929–1945.* New York: Oxford University Press, 1999, p. 104.

4. Allan Nevins and Henry Steele Commager, *A Pocket History of the United States.* 9th ed. New York: Pocket Books, 1992, p. 418.

Chapter 1: Growing Up a Roosevelt

5. Quoted in Ted Morgan, *FDR: A Biography.* New York: Simon & Schuster, 1985, p. 47.

6. Quoted in Morgan, *FDR*, p. 39.

7. Quoted in Doris Kearns Goodwin, "Franklin Delano Roosevelt," *Time*, December 31, 1999, p. 96.

8. Geoffrey C. Ward, *Before the Trumpet: Young Franklin Roosevelt 1882–1905.* New York: Harper & Row, 1985, p. 110.

9. James Roosevelt, *My Parents: A Differing View.* Chicago: Playboy Press, 1976, p. 28.

10. Quoted in Ward, *Before the Trumpet*, p. 180.

11. Quoted in Robert Shogan, *The Double-Edged Sword: How Character Makes and Ruins Presidents, from Washington to Clinton.* Boulder, CO: Westview Press, 1999, p. 79.

12. Quoted in Morgan, *FDR*, p. 58.

13. Quoted in Joseph P. Lash, *Eleanor and Franklin: The Story of Their Relationship, Based on Eleanor Roosevelt's Private Papers.* New York: W.W. Norton, 1971, p. 28.

14. Quoted in Lash, *Eleanor and Franklin*, p. 43.

15. Quoted in Public Broadcasting System, "The American Experience: Eleanor Roosevelt," 1999. www.pbs.org/wgbh/amex/eleanor/filmmore/transcript/index.html.

16. Quoted in Roosevelt, *My Parents*, p. 21.

17. Quoted in Ward, *Before the Trumpet*, p. 260.

18. Quoted in Lash, *Eleanor and Franklin*, p. xiv.

Chapter 2: Early Success, Then Tragedy

19. Quoted in Roosevelt, *My Parents*, p. 19.

20. Quoted in Kenneth S. Davis, *FDR: The Beckoning of Destiny, 1882–1928.* New York: G. P. Putnam's Sons, 1972, p. 214.

21. Quoted in James MacGregor Burns, *Roosevelt: The Lion and the Fox.* New York: Harcourt, Brace & World, 1956, p. 32.

22. Burns, *Roosevelt*, p. 40.

23. Quoted in Burns, *Roosevelt*, p. 50.

24. Quoted in Frank Freidel, *Franklin D. Roosevelt: A Rendezvous with Destiny.* Boston: Little, Brown, 1990, p. 14.

25. Quoted in Lash, *Eleanor and Franklin*, p. 91.

26. Quoted in Public Broadcasting System, "The American Experience: Eleanor Roosevelt."

27. Roosevelt, *My Parents*, p. 101.

28. Quoted in Doris Kearns Goodwin, *No Ordinary Time: Franklin and Eleanor Roosevelt: The Home Front in World War II.* New York: Simon & Schuster, 1994, p. 19.

29. Quoted in Morgan, *FDR*, p. 227.

30. Quoted in Morgan, *FDR*, p. 230.

31. Quoted in Davis, *FDR*, p. 648.

32. Quoted in Freidel, *Franklin D. Roosevelt: A Rendezvous with Destiny*, p. 41.

33. Quoted in Davis, *FDR*, p. 651.

Chapter 3: Overcoming Polio and Making a Political Comeback

34. Quoted in Geoffrey C. Ward, *A First-Class Temperament: The Emergence of Franklin Roosevelt*. New York: Harper & Row, 1989, p. 630.

35. Quoted in Hugh Gregory Gallagher, *FDR's Splendid Deception*. New York: Dodd, Mead, 1985, p. 26.

36. Quoted in "The American President." http://216.132.160.230/KoTrain/Courses/FDR/FDR_In_Brief.html.

37. Quoted in Gallagher, *FDR's Splendid Deception*, p. 36.

38. Gallagher, *FDR's Splendid Deception*, p. xi.

39. Quoted in Morgan, *FDR*, p. 259.

40. Quoted in Public Broadcasting System, "The American Experience: Eleanor Roosevelt."

41. Burns, *Roosevelt*, p. 89.

42. Davis, *FDR*, p. 681.

43. Quoted in Lash, *Eleanor and Franklin*, p. 276.

44. Quoted in Ward, *A First-Class Temperament*, p. 688.

45. Quoted in Lash, *Eleanor and Franklin*, p. 135.

46. Quoted in Morgan, *FDR*, p. 259.

47. Roosevelt, *My Parents*, p. 91.

48. Quoted in Burns, *Roosevelt*, p. 101.

49. Quoted in Frank Freidel, *Franklin D. Roosevelt: Launching the New Deal*. Boston: Little, Brown, 1973, p. 55.

50. Quoted in Morgan, *FDR*, p. 322.

51. Quoted in Gallagher, *FDR's Splendid Deception*, p. 94.

52. Gallagher, *FDR's Splendid Deception*, p. xiv.

53. Quoted in Miller, *F.D.R.*, p. 279.

Chapter 4: FDR's First Term: Battling the Great Depression

54. Quoted in Arthur M. Schlesinger Jr., *The Age of Roosevelt: The Crisis of the Old Order 1919–1933*. Boston: Houghton Mifflin, 1957, p. 3.

55. Quoted in the Program in Presidential Rhetoric at Texas A&M University. www.tamu.edu/scom/pres/pres.html

56. Quoted in James West Davidson et al., *Nation of Nations: A Narrative History of the American Republic*. 2nd ed. New York: McGraw-Hill, 1994, p. 414.

57. Robert Kelley, *The Shaping of the American Past*. Vol. 2, 5th ed. Englewood Cliffs, NJ: Prentice-Hall, 1990, p. 595.

58. Quoted in Kennedy, *Freedom from Fear*, p. 33.

59. Quoted in Samuel Eliot Morison, *The Oxford History of the American People*. New York: Oxford University Press, 1965, p. 945.

60. Quoted in Miller, *F.D.R.*, p. 288.

61. Quoted in Kennedy, *Freedom from Fear*, p. 100.

62. Quoted in the Program in Presidential Rhetoric at Texas A&M University.

63. Quoted in Miller, *F.D.R.*, p. 311.

64. Quoted in Goodwin, "Franklin D. Roosevelt."

65. Quoted in the Program in Presidential Rhetoric at Texas A&M University.

66. Quoted in Kennedy, *Freedom from Fear*, p. 262.

Chapter 5: FDR's Second Term: Battling His Enemies

67. Quoted in Goodwin, "Franklin Delano Roosevelt," p. 98.

68. Quoted in Burns, *Roosevelt*, p. 271.

69. Quoted in Burns, *Roosevelt*, p. 274.

70. Quoted in Miller, *F.D.R.*, p. 384.

71. Quoted in Cabell Phillips, *From the Crash to the Blitz: 1929–1939*. Toronto, Ontario, Canada: Macmillan, 1969, p. 489.

72. Quoted in Frank Freidel, *Franklin D. Roosevelt: Launching the New Deal*, p. 503.

73. Quoted in Miller, *F.D.R.*, p. 399.

74. Phillips, *From the Crash to the Blitz*, p. 504.

75. Quoted in Morison, *The Oxford History of the American People*, p. 979.

76. Quoted in Michael P. Riccards, *The Ferocious Engine of Democracy: A History of the American Presidency*. Vol. 2. New York: Madison Books, 1995, p. 154.

77. Quoted in Morison, *The Oxford History of the American People*, p. 346.

78. Quoted in Kennedy, *Freedom from Fear*, p. 405.

79. Quoted in Kennedy, *Freedom from Fear*, p. 406.

80. Quoted in Morgan, *FDR*, p. 510.

81. Quoted in Miller, *F.D.R.*, p. 453.

Chapter 6: FDR's Third Term: Battling Isolationists

82. Quoted in Roosevelt, *My Parents*, p. 160.

83. Quoted in Burns, *Roosevelt*, p. 440.

84. Quoted in William Manchester, *The Glory and the Dream: A Narrative History of America 1932–1972*. Boston: Little, Brown, 1974, p. 273.

85. Quoted in Miller, *F.D.R.*, p. 457.

86. Quoted in Kennedy, *Freedom from Fear*, p. 463.

87. Quoted in Manchester, *The Glory and the Dream*, p. 278.

88. Quoted in Miller, *F.D.R.*, p. 461.

89. Quoted in the Program in Presidential Rhetoric at Texas A&M University.

90. Quoted in Miller, *F.D.R.*, p. 463.

91. Quoted in Freidel, *Franklin D. Roosevelt: A Rendezvous with Destiny*, p. 29.

92. Quoted in Kelley, *The Shaping of the American Past*, p. 645.

93. Quoted in the Program in Presidential Rhetoric at Texas A&M University.

94. Quoted in Manchester, *The Glory and the Dream*, p. 313.

95. Quoted in Kennedy, *Freedom from Fear*, p. 526.

96. Miller, *F.D.R.*, p. 481.

97. Roosevelt, *My Parents*, p. 251.

98. Quoted in Goodwin, *No Ordinary Time*, p. 20.

99. Quoted in Goodwin, "Franklin D. Roosevelt."

Chapter 7: Winning a War, Striving for Peace

100. Quoted in Freidel, *Franklin D. Roosevelt: A Rendezvous with Destiny*, p. 39.

101. Quoted in Kennedy, *Freedom from Fear*, p. 691.

102. Quoted in Manchester, *The Glory and the Dream*, p. 354.

103. Quoted in Goodwin, *No Ordinary Time*, p. 246.

104. Quoted in Freidel, *Franklin D. Roosevelt: A Rendezvous with Destiny*, p. 415.

105. Quoted in Freidel, *Franklin D. Roosevelt: A Rendezvous with Destiny*, p. 455.

106. Quoted in Morgan, *FDR*, p. 691.

107. Quoted in the Mid-Hudson Regional Information Center. www.mhric.org/fdr/chat27.html.

108. Quoted in Davidson et al., *Nation of Nations*, p. 1,036.

109. Quoted in Miller, *F.D.R.*, p. 501.

110. Quoted in Jim Bishop, *FDR's Last Year: April 1944–April 1945*. New York: William Morrow, 1974, p. 267.

111. Quoted in Goodwin, *No Ordinary Time*, p. 807.

112. Quoted in Bishop, *FDR's Last Year*, p. 473.

113. Quoted in Manchester, *The Glory and the Dream*, p. 426.

114. Quoted in Freidel, *Franklin D. Roosevelt: A Rendezvous with Destiny*, p. 605.

Epilogue: FDR's Curious Legacy

115. Quoted in Goodwin, "Franklin Delano Roosevelt," p. 98.

116. Quoted in Bishop, *FDR's Last Year*, p. 616.

117. Quoted in E. J. Dionne Jr., "Roosevelt, America's Original Man from Hope," *Washington Post*, May 1, 1997, p. C1.

118. Quoted in Miller, *F.D.R.*, p. 506.

119. Quoted in Freidel, *Franklin D. Roosevelt: A Rendezvous with Destiny*, p. 601.

120. Riccards, *The Ferocious Engine of Democracy*, p. xvii.

121. Morgan, *FDR*, p. 772.

122. William J. Clinton, "Remarks on the Unveiling of a Statue at the Franklin D. Roosevelt Memorial," *Weekly Compilation of Presidential Documents*, January 15, 2001, p. 70.

123. Quoted in Burns, *Roosevelt*, p. 423.

For Further Reading

Marcus Cunliffe and the Editors of *American Heritage, The American Heritage History of the Presidency*. New York: Simon & Schuster, 1968. A book that explains how various presidents have changed the presidency by the way they governed.

Hugh Gregory Gallagher, *FDR's Splendid Deception*. New York: Dodd, Mead, 1985. The author, a polio victim himself, explains how Roosevelt coped with his illness and how it affected him.

Joseph Gies, *Franklin D. Roosevelt: Portrait of a President*. Garden City, NY: Doubleday, 1971. A solid biography of Roosevelt for younger readers.

Robert Kelley, *The Shaping of the American Past*. Vol. 2, 5th ed. Englewood Cliffs, NJ: Prentice-Hall, 1990. An excellent history book that includes valuable insights into why and how events happened as they did.

Nathan Miller, *F.D.R.: An Intimate History*. Garden City, NY: Doubleday, 1983. This biography of Roosevelt details his personal life as well as the important things he did as a public figure.

Ted Morgan, *FDR: A Biography*. New York: Simon & Schuster, 1985. A straightforward, concise telling of Roosevelt's life that also puts his accomplishments into perspective.

Allan Nevins and Henry Steele Commager, *A Pocket History of the United States*. 9th ed. New York: Pocket Books, 1992. A brief, concise explanation of U.S. history loaded with not only facts but insights into why important events happened.

Cabell Phillips, *From the Crash to the Blitz: 1929–1939*. Toronto, Ontario, Canada: Macmillan, 1969. An entertaining yet informative look at the Great Depression and how it affected American life.

Michael V. Uschan, *A Cultural History of the United States Through the Decades: The 1940s*. San Diego: Lucent Books, 1999. A comprehensive look at how Americans lived in one of the most important decades in their history.

Works Consulted

Books

Jim Bishop, *FDR's Last Year: April 1944–April 1945*. New York: William Morrow, 1974. A detailed account of Roosevelt's final year, including the events that took place at Yalta.

James MacGregor Burns, *Roosevelt: The Lion and the Fox*. New York: Harcourt, Brace & World, 1956. This respected historian explains Roosevelt's life and considers his accomplishments in perspective with those of other presidents.

James West Davidson et al., *Nation of Nations: A Narrative History of the American Republic*. 2nd ed. New York: McGraw-Hill, 1994. A readable, insightful explanation of U.S. history.

Kenneth S. Davis, *FDR: The Beckoning of Destiny, 1882–1928*. New York: G.P. Putnam's Sons, 1972. Davis, who has written extensively on Roosevelt, explains Roosevelt's life up until his election as governor in 1928.

Frank Freidel, *Franklin D. Roosevelt: A Rendezvous with Destiny*. Boston: Little, Brown, 1990. An insightful biography of Roosevelt by an author who has written extensively on the subject.

——, *Franklin D. Roosevelt: Launching the New Deal*. Boston: Little, Brown, 1973. The author deals with Roosevelt's first term when he began to fight the Great Depression.

Doris Kearns Goodwin, *No Ordinary Time: Franklin and Eleanor Roosevelt: The Home Front in World War II*. New York: Simon & Schuster, 1994. This Pulitzer Prize–winning author delves into the lives of this famous couple during the war years.

David M. Kennedy, *Freedom from Fear: The American People in Depression and War, 1929–1945*. New York: Oxford University Press, 1999. An excellent account of what happened in America during this pivotal period in U.S. history.

Joseph P. Lash, *Eleanor and Franklin: The Story of Their Relationship, Based on Eleanor Roosevelt's Private Papers*. New York: W.W. Norton, 1971. A close friend of Eleanor, the author used his access to family documents to write this book.

William Manchester, *The Glory and the Dream: A Narrative History of America 1932–1972*. Boston: Little, Brown, 1974. A book more concerned with explaining to readers what it was like to live during this period than interpreting the events that took place.

Samuel Eliot Morison, *The Oxford History of the American People*. New York: Oxford University Press, 1965. A fine history of the United States that also explains America's relationship with the rest of the world.

Michael P. Riccards, *The Ferocious Engine of Democracy: A History of the American Presidency*. Vol. 2. New York: Madison Books, 1995. The author explains how history has shaped the presidency and how presidents have shaped history.

James Roosevelt, *My Parents: A Differing View*. Chicago: Playboy Press, 1976. He writes about his parents and what it was like growing up the son of two very famous people.

Arthur M. Schlesinger Jr., *The Age of Roosevelt: The Crisis of the Old Order 1919–1933*. Boston: Houghton Mifflin, 1957. In this first of four volumes on Roosevelt, the Pulitzer Prize–winning author details an important part of his subject's life.

Robert Shogan, *The Double-Edged Sword: How Character Makes and Ruins Presidents, from Washington to Clinton*. Boulder, CO: Westview Press, 1999. An interesting look at how various chief executives have influenced the presidency.

Geoffrey C. Ward, *A First-Class Temperament: The Emergence of Franklin Roosevelt*. New York: Harper & Row, 1989. This noted Roosevelt biographer looks at his subject's early political successes.

———, *Before the Trumpet: Young Franklin Roosevelt 1882–1905*. New York: Harper & Row, 1985. A detailed look at Roosevelt's early life by one of Roosevelt's finest biographers.

Periodicals

William J. Clinton, "Remarks on the Unveiling of a Statue at the Franklin D. Roosevelt Memorial," *Weekly Compilation of Presidential Documents*, January 15, 2001.

E. J. Dionne Jr., "Roosevelt, America's Original Man from Hope," *Washington Post*, May 1, 1997.

Doris Kearns Goodwin, "Franklin Delano Roosevelt," *Time*, December 31, 1999.

Internet Sources

"The American President." http://216.132.160.230/KoTrain/Courses/FDR/FDR_In_Brief.html. This Internet site is based on the Public Broadcasting System television series that aired on April 9, 2000. The site was developed in coordination with the National Council for Social Studies.

Franklin and Eleanor Roosevelt Institute (FERI). www.feri.org/fdr/speech03.html. This website has biographical information on the Roosevelts as well as many of Franklin's speeches.

Doris Kearns Goodwin, "Franklin D. Roosevelt." www.pbs.org/newshour/character/essays/roosevelt.html. Excerpts from an essay on Roosevelt's character by the Pulitzer Prize–winning historian.

Landon Lecture Series at Kansas State University. http://gos.sbc.edu/g/goodwin.html. A speech on Franklin Delano Roosevelt delivered on April 22, 1997, by Doris Kearns Goodwin.

Mid-Hudson Regional Information Center. www.mhric.org/fdr/chat27.html. The MHRIC in New York state has on-line material available for school districts, including many of President Roosevelt's speeches and fireside chats.

Program in Presidential Rhetoric at Texas A&M University. www.tamu.edu/scom/pres/pres.html. This website has an archive of the texts of historic presidential speeches.

Public Broadcasting System. www.pbs.org/wgbh/amex/truman/psources/ps_einstein.html. This site has information on many areas of U.S. history.

Public Broadcasting System, "The American Experience: Eleanor Roosevelt," 1999. www.pbs.org/wgbh/amex/eleanor/filmmore/transcript/index.html. An enhanced transcript of the show aired in 1999.

Index

Picture Credits

About the Author

Michael V. Uschan has written nearly twenty books, including biographies of President John F. Kennedy and Minnesota governor Jesse Ventura and *America's Founders*, a collective biography of five historical figures who founded the nation. Mr. Uschan began his career as a writer and editor with United Press International, a wire service that provides stories to newspapers, radio, and television. Journalism is sometimes called "history in a hurry." Mr. Uschan considers writing history books a natural extension of the skills he developed in his many years as a working journalist. He and his wife, Barbara, reside in the Milwaukee suburb of Franklin, Wisconsin.